FOUR-

LEGGED

THERAPY

dept.store *for* the mind

FOUR-LEGGED THERAPY

HOW FUR, SCALES AND FEATHERS CAN MAKE LIFE WORTH LIVING

aster

An Hachette UK Company
www.hachette.co.uk

First published in Great Britain in 2018 by Aster,
an imprint of Octopus Publishing Group Ltd
Carmelite House
50 Victoria Embankment
London EC4Y 0DZ
www.octopusbooks.co.uk

Distributed in the US by Hachette Book Group
1290 Avenue of the Americas
4th and 5th Floors
New York, NY 10104

Distributed in Canada by Canadian Manda Group
664 Annette St.
Toronto, Ontario,
Canada M6S 2C8

ISBN 978 1 91202 366 0

A CIP catalogue record for this book is available
from the British Library.

Printed and bound in China

10 9 8 7 6 5 4 3 2 1

Consultant Publisher Kate Adams
Consultant Editors Ruth Williams and Katie Steel
Senior Editor Pollyanna Poulter
Copy Editor Alison Wormleighton
Senior Designer Jaz Bahra at Octopus
Creative Direction and Design: Katie Steel,
Jo Raynsford and Rochelle Maas at Supafrank
Illustrator Veronica Wood
Photography James Champion
Cat Photograph on page 47 Susannah Conway
Production Manager Caroline Alberti

Disclaimer/Publisher's note
All reasonable care has been taken in the
preparation of this book, but the information
it contains is not intended to take the place of
treatment by a qualified medical practitioner.

dept.store *for* the mind

Each book offers stories and ideas about creating daily habits that are kind
to the mind, whether through our connection with nature, our creativity or
everyday tasks, or simply knowing and feeling more accepting of ourselves.
The books stretch the mind and soul, so that we may colour outside the
lines, experience the moments of wonder that are right there in front
of us and occasionally venture out of our safe harbours.

Department Store for the Mind is an exciting new creative venture
offering a place to explore the world inside your head: a vast and
unique terrain of thoughts, ideas, emotions and memories.

www.deptstoreforthemind.com

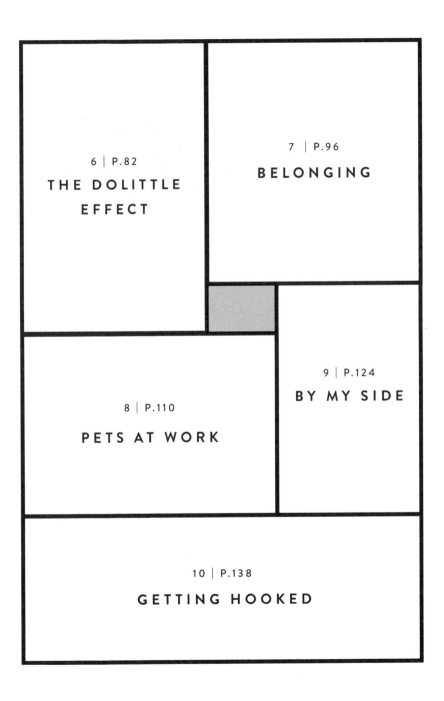

KATIE AT CORRINGHAM PET SHOW, 1986

INTRODUCTION

Katie Steel | Creative Director and
Co-owner of Department Store for the Mind

Four years ago, my sister Rebecca sent me a picture of a pretty little collie posing neatly with my two nephews – ears flat, eyes staring into the camera. This was the first time I saw Nell.

Two weeks later, Tom and I set off to pick her up from my uncle's house. Nell greeted us in the kitchen with a downward-facing dog. I tickled her ears, she wagged silently, then hid under the table.

Having grown up around collies, I thought a three-year-old Nell would be bouncy and reckless around our home, so I had bought baby gates and covered anything that was precious to me. When she trotted into the living room though, delicately sniffed around, then laid down flat on her side with a little smile, I was amazed and relieved. She had definitely found her home and somehow knew it.

Nell and I get each other – both of us are naturally obsessive, unblinkingly determined and need one another to remember to pause. We go on walks together and she runs alongside my wheels on bike rides for totally joyful hours. Nell sits at my feet as I work, contented – banging her tail loudly on the floor when it is time to go home. She sits with, or lays on me if I am struggling with something and genuinely makes me laugh every day.

Nell fits perfectly into our world and I have become happier – lighter somehow. Is it just the companionship and love, or is there more to it?

Can our four-legged friends really help with our mental health?

CHAPTER 1

FOUR-
LEGGED
THERAPY

FOUR-LEGGED THERAPY

How your pet can be good for you

Sophie Rickard | Psychologist, Writer, Author of *Mann's Best Friend*

The last thing I expected to find on a misty hillside was a sudden, intense surge of joy.

It was an eerily still day in November. My Border collie, Jessie, and I were herding a small flock of well-behaved training sheep through a simple course. I felt a powerful bond of love and trust between us; an intense understanding that was about more than just rearranging sheep. We glowed.

I need to give this miracle some context. I am very much an "indoors toy". I have a painful health condition that exhausts me and restricts my mobility. Most of my interaction takes place online. I have always been bookish, and have struggled with social anxiety since a breakdown five years ago that left me agoraphobic, terrified and paranoid. Lots of things have helped me get better, but what brought me to that particular moment on that hillside was four-legged therapy.

WHAT IS THERAPY?

It depends who you ask. For me, therapy includes anything that helps you to be more You. We each have inside us the potential to feel calm and be amazing – even simultaneously. But sometimes it can be hard for this potential to find its way to the surface. Therapy allows us to nurture the potential and help it to find the light.

Domestic animals offer the perfect conditions for therapy. (I am not excluding the healing powers of birds, fish, snakes or three-legged cats here. I mean to

" "

THERAPY
INCLUDES
ANYTHING
THAT HELPS
YOU TO BE
MORE YOU

include them all. We are not all in a position to share our lives with a horse, or a dog, or even a hamster, but even the tiniest city rental has space for a window bird feeder – and with it the joy of a friendly face in the mornings.) A well-loved pet is part of the family, yet offers some things that friends and family cannot. They love you unconditionally and show affection without restraint. They can read you better than you can yourself. And they are always honest. That's all it takes. This might seem like a bit of a stretch, but humour me.

What about "talking cures"? In popular imagination, therapy means lying on a couch and talking about childhood – this is Freudian psychoanalysis. I respect Freud's genius, but let's remember that he treated his own emotional pain with cocaine and occasionally slept through client sessions, so nobody's perfect. Do you talk to the cat? Do you sing to the budgie, or reassure the dog that the postman is *allowed* to walk up the path? We are verbal with our pets, and for the most part they do not make verbal responses. But we don't mind, because we know we have been heard.

"CAN ANYONE REALLY HEAR YOU, THROUGH THE THICK, WOOLLY FILTER OF THEIR OWN THOUGHTS, FEELINGS, PREJUDICES, PREDISPOSITIONS AND RELATIVE SOCIAL POSITION?"

I find that people can be *too* verbal. How does it feel to be presented with solutions, when all you want is a good old moan? Are there things you daren't discuss for fear of gossip? Is it insensitive to offload to a friend who has their own, apparently more pressing, burdens? Can anyone really *hear* you, through the thick, woolly filter of their own thoughts, feelings, prejudices, predispositions and relative social position? The cat can. He may not understand the finer points of your existential crisis, but he does care. He also allows you to talk, and you may well find you hear yourself saying things that surprise you.

THE MAGIC INGREDIENTS

According to Carl Rogers, the father of person-centred counselling (the sort that believes the answers are all inside you, waiting to be let out), there are three key components for therapy to work: empathy, honesty and love. That's not much to ask. And it is this simplicity and faith in the human capacity for brilliance that draws me to the person-centred school of thought. But how easy is it to find a no-strings space in our modern lives where empathy, honesty and love are made available? A context that offers these elements is a sacred space to be treasured, because that is where magic can happen.

At a high-security prison in Cape Town, South Africa, the lives of notorious murderers and rapists have been transformed by lovebirds. In a unique rehabilitation programme, the prisoners hatch and hand-rear chicks, to be sold as pets after ten weeks. One of them said, "I now realize what my wife went through with our five children, while I did nothing to help. I wake up naturally in the night because I know these birds need me. Without me, they would die. I think it will help me be a better parent when I get out." For some inmates, the bond with the bird is the first loving relationship they have experienced, and it is life changing.

Empathy

Empathy and sympathy are not the same thing. Sympathy is someone feeling sadness or pity for your situation, while empathy is when they recognize how a situation makes you feel, and feel a shade of that emotion alongside you. It is a vital part of any therapeutic relationship, and it is something pets do in bucketloads. You are important to them, and they sense when you are distressed or in pain. They show it through silent affection: a warm head resting on your knee, or a lick of the fingers. My son calls Jessie's generous expressions of solidarity "puppy powers".

We empathize with our pets too. How does your companion tell you when he is under the weather? He doesn't have to. You know him so well you can just tell. It is instinctive to reassure him when he is frightened, to share in the pure joy of a new tennis ball, or commiserate with a bad tummy. This stuff is not complicated. It seems to come naturally.

" "

HOW DOES IT FEEL
TO BE PRESENTED WITH
SOLUTIONS, WHEN ALL
YOU WANT IS A GOOD
OLD MOAN?

Honesty

Honesty is also essential for therapy. To wholeheartedly *be* with someone means being real, open, flexible, and without distortion or denial. This is a tall order for people. We are hyperaware of the social cues we are constantly "leaking" (Do I look professional? Did I sound foolish? Am I acting too needy?). To live inside your own skin, without judgment or attempts at self-improvement, is the realm of the Zen master. Yet I think I might achieve it for a few private moments each day, when I am with Jessie. She knows the whole me, and I am comfortable with that.

Do you lie to your pet? This is a source of vigorous debate in our house. Perhaps there is a place for comforting lies, like, "Let's go for a walk [to the vet's]", or, "She'll be back soon [after a year abroad]". Maybe it's different for animals with less language comprehension than a curious Border collie. But there is something so pure and innocent in the trust animals give us that makes me uncomfortable with untruths. I try to be honest. It helps me to be aware of any times I am tempted not to be.

Love

If you can combine empathy and honesty with love, you have the magical conditions for growth.

There are different kinds of love. I am not talking about *eros* (romantic, sexual love) or *philia* (brotherly, shared-duty kind of love), but of *agape*. English does not seem to have a word for this form of pure and gentle goodwill, benevolence and wilful delight in another. This love is unconditional and without judgment. It incorporates both respect and faith in each person's capacity to be amazing. And it is what you see when your dog gazes into your eyes.

Have you ever accidentally witnessed the private intimacy and pure delight when a person and their pet greet one another? It is a window onto absolute adoration on both sides, framed by the free affection that a non-judgmental relationship liberates. I don't know about you, but I am more regularly, casually and warmly physically affectionate with my dog than I am with any adult human. Jessie seems always to be ready for a cuddle.

Some people respond well to therapy that includes lots of goal-setting and instructions. Cognitive behavioural therapy works brilliantly for lots of behavioural issues, like phobias and fears; it can be amazing when a professional suggests coping strategies and gives you new things to think about. For others, long-term, deep analysis of their subconscious can help them make changes and be happier. Your tortoise cannot provide any of these things. But I, as a person-centred counsellor, would not provide them either. I would offer you time, space, empathy, honesty and *agape* love. And let you do the rest.

PETS ARE GOOD FOR YOU

In that case, could a robot be just as good? Sony's interactive robotic dog, AIBO, is marketed as a "social companion" and researchers were keen to find out whether it could offer a clean, safe substitute for animal-assisted therapy. They gave a group of children two play sessions: one with AIBO, the other with an unfamiliar, but friendly, real dog. The children offered the dog nearly five times more affection, and many spent the entire play session (and the interview) snuggling her. Children see pets as friends and family members. In the study, they found it easy to transfer this status to the real dog, but not so much to AIBO. Although they found AIBO to be a mediocre dog substitute, the children offered some fascinating reasons why it could be better than the real thing:

- "The robotic dog would never die, and so I would never be sad."

- "We would save money on dog food and doctor visits."

- "I could take AIBO to school and with me everywhere."

What I hear in these statements is loss. But they could be translated as:

- What if we dare to love someone and they leave us?

- What if we don't have enough to give?

- What if we must be separated?

This is what it is to be human. To feel, and to yearn. It seems that a relationship with AIBO would be an opportunity to sidestep these risky but vital questions.

Pets are good for you. This is an established scientific idea, widely accepted across lots of disciplines and well documented. Keeping dogs or horses, in particular, means lots of exercise and outdoor fun you might not otherwise have. A Swedish study looked at the health and wellbeing of more than 3 million people over the course of 12 years. They poked about in people's health records for all kinds of factors, and one of the things they noted was whether or not they kept a dog. They found dog ownership to be "inversely associated" with dying. So do dogs not only improve the *quality* of our lives, but also keep the Grim Reaper away? No, it would be silly to claim that dogs keep you alive for ever, and that's not what they found. The study showed that dog owners were less likely than the dogless to die during the 12-year study. This was particularly the case for single people living alone, who had a 33 percent lower risk of death if they had a dog.

And here's a thing: the dog breeds most closely linked to this "protective effect" were hunting dogs – including terriers, retrievers, scent hounds – with pointers topping the charts. Long live pointers and their companions!

But what caught my attention, as a disabled person who finds exercise difficult, was that the researchers did not put this finding completely down to exercise. They did talk about "cardiovascular health benefits" – in other words, avoiding heart attacks, high blood pressure and stroke. But it wasn't all down to the walking. They said that "psychosocial stress factors" (including social isolation, depression and loneliness) were all lower in dog owners. They talked about the nervous system and explained that lower reactivity to stress, and faster recovery following stressful events were also associated with dog ownership.

Can it really be that spending time with Jessie helps lower my anxiety levels, even though someone else does the walking? I know that going outside is good for me, but I don't manage it every day. Sometimes I have to choose carefully how I will spend the limited energy at my disposal, and stomping through fields in the rain doesn't always make the cut. So what is it that she is providing that has such a good influence on my mood?

HOW DOES IT WORK, REALLY?

Our pets are great communicators, if we care to listen. Dogs are even better at using human social cues than our closest relatives, chimpanzees. This could be because domestic dogs have evolved alongside humans to understand and interact with the "human pack". For example, you can point your finger to direct a dog's attention. Dogs are also great at using mutual gaze to get your help. Jessie can make herself heard without talking or pointing with her paws. She directs my attention to the door that needs opening, or the biscuits that need eating, with her eyes.

A researcher in Japan looked into the chemistry behind a dog's loving gaze. He and his team (including Anita and Jasmine, his standard poodles) discovered a positive feedback loop between people and dogs. In humans, mutual gaze is a sign of bonding between mother and baby, and also between sexual partners. The hormone oxytocin increases with this eye contact. Raised oxytocin seems to make us feel calmer and inclined to snuggle. You can see how this might have helped evolution along – by encouraging us to make babies, then want to keep them close. But the study found that it works with our pet dogs too. Time spent gazing into the eyes of your dog is a chemical stress reliever, for both of you.

I spend a lot of time thinking about chronic pain, although I wish I didn't. It's not a great idea for me to use pharmaceutical pain relief all the time, because of side effects and because it's not so safe for long-term use. So I look for other ways to manage my response to pain, including mindfulness and distraction. Jessie seems to have a special gift for sensing which part of my body is painful, and sacrificing her own comfort to act as a canine hot-water bottle, draping herself over me accordingly. I also appreciate the time she spends just being with me when I'm stuck in bed or on the sofa.

"The animal–human connection is powerful in reducing stress and in generating a sense of wellbeing," says Julia Havey, the lead researcher in a hospital-based study that looked into pain relief. People recovering from total joint replacements (such as new hips or knees) enjoyed short, daily hospital visits from specially trained dogs – five to 15 minutes of chatting, stroking and gentle interaction on the ward. The people who took part in this "animal-assisted intervention" needed 28 percent less pain-relief medicine than their dog-starved counterparts. How can it be that patting a dog for 10 minutes could cut analgesic use by more than a quarter? Maybe it's oxytocin from all the gazing? Or it could be physical affection that does it. I just wonder whether this is another example of the unexpected power of empathy, honesty and love.

Animal-assisted therapy is well established in many parts of the world. If you think you and your dog could provide this miracle service to others, look into pet-therapy services in your area. Not all pets can be that competent, with or without special training; let's face it, some animals are positively grumpy. But when we choose to share our lives with them, we are entering into a long-term, close relationship of interdependence.

So that's how Jessie brought me to that misty hillside. I was a good mile out of my comfort zone, feeling cold, dizzy and exhausted. I was bemused by the essential pointlessness of the sheep arranging, but it was clear that Jessie was born to herd. She had persuaded me, using the force of the *agape* between us, to get outdoors and try something new. And we experienced what athletes call flow. We were in the zone, together. I'm certain it was neither graceful nor technically well done, but we felt the thrill of achievement together. And our relationship has been closer and stronger ever since. Using empathy, honesty and love, Jessie and I expanded the universe that day.

I'm not saying that life with pets has no drawbacks. Any relationship that involves quite this much poo ought to be questioned. Neither am I suggesting that all you need to recover from trauma is a chinchilla – never mind that prescription from your doctor. What I mean is, if you look closely, your pets are offering you the perfect conditions for a therapeutic relationship.

There is a world of support waiting to sit on your lap.

PAWS FOR THOUGHT

Living and loving with your pets

1 | INGREDIENTS

The conditions to facilitate personal growth are empathy, honesty and love. Look for these in your relationships. Try offering them to others. Be real.

2 | EMPATHY

Be aware of your internal empathic responses. Listen to them, and consider sharing them with the object of your empathy. We all feel alone with our struggles sometimes.

3 | HONESTY

Think about "being yourself" and the different selves you enlist in different circumstances. Is the You that your pet knows the most comfortable one? What makes it so?

4 | LOVE

Be aware of the different kinds of love. Look for *agape* in your life. Where you would like to see *agape* love grow? Plant some seedlings of your own. Water them.

5 | LOSS

To love is a risk. Try to be aware of that without being frightened away. Loss is all around us, and it is what makes love so vital.

6 | FUN

Enjoy spending time with animals. Soak up all that oxytocin and pain relief! Have fun – you know it is good for you both.

CHAPTER 2

UNCONDITIONAL

LIKE

CHAPTER 2

UNCONDITIONAL LIKE

Learning to like yourself, warts and all

Caroline O'Donoghue | Author of *Promising Young Women*
and Editor at websites The Pool and White Noise

Whether the night has been good or not, the morning is always the same. Whether I have spent the night tossing and turning – practising my breathing, practising switching off, practising not looking at my phone – or whether I have been soundly asleep, she always says good morning in exactly the same way. By bounding out of the living room, skittering her paws along the corridor and leaping her tiny white body onto the bed. She spares a brief moment for formalities: her "Did you sleep well?" is a lick on the chin; her "Any plans for today, then?" is an attempt to stick her nose in my mouth while I yawn. Sometimes, I am working off four hours of interrupted sleep. Sometimes, I have had a full, rested eight. But the morning is always the same.

Sylvie is a Jack Russell terrier. People who like Jack Russells are very passionate about defending them; people who do not like Jack Russells are very keen to tell you why, exactly, they are not to be trusted. Both fans and foes of the Jack Russell have the same crux in their argument: if you like them, it's because they have a lot of character; if you don't, it's because they have too much character. There is a fine line between being charming and being "a bit much". I move over and across that line every day.

When we went to view the litter that Sylvie came from, she was a pop-eyed, white-haired alien, running literal circles around a family of docile black-and-tan pups. She had conjunctivitis in both eyes and was also being treated for worms. Try telling her that, though. As far as she was concerned, she was the pick of the bunch.

" "

YOUR DOG'S UTTER
FAITH IN YOUR
HUMANITY WILL
MAKE YOU FEEL
LIKE MORE AND
MORE OF A HUMAN,
EVERY DAY

We reached down and lifted her up. She was the exact size and weight of a baked potato. She squealed with happiness, and tried to get closer, closer, to live inside of us, if she could.

"I love her," my partner said, his voice cracking with joy. "But she is a bit extra, isn't she?"

A LITTLE EXTRA

This is Sylvie's most Jack-Russell trait of all: she's just a bit extra. A bit much. If she were a person, people might think twice about inviting her to a party: "Oh, she's a good laugh, but I'm not sure I'm quite up for that, tonight," they would say, and reasonably so.

"I WANT SOMETHING THAT FEELS THE SAME WAY ABOUT ME EVERY DAY"

Some people don't want a dog that tries to climb inside their mouths. It turns out that (to our great surprise) we *are* the sort of people who want a dog that climbs inside our mouths. Horses for courses; terriers for teeth.

I'm a bit extra too, I think. That isn't some kind of subtle brag. I barge into conversations. I'm not always kind. I have not read enough. I strongly suspect that there are a great many dinner parties I have not been invited to, or was almost invited to, because the person hosting thought I was a little bit much. A laugh, sure. But are we in the mood for all that tonight?

These are the thoughts that unsettle me, unmoor me in the night. I stare at the back of my partner's head as he snoozes and I think of more things I'm doing wrong. These feelings have intensified since last year, when I started making my living as a full-time freelance writer. I quit my job to focus on my novels, and, I thought, to live a creative bohemian life filled with gallery openings and flatteringly oversized shirt-dresses. I thought that I needed more time to write, but judging by the fact that I am writing the exact same amount of fiction a day as I was when I had a full-time job, that theory is proving untrue. I need routine. I am no longer protected by the consistency of an everyday workplace, a place where I know who likes me and who doesn't.

In the world of a jobbing freelancer, people's opinions of you can fluctuate on a daily basis. You write a piece. Strangers tell you they love it. Your editor congratulates you on your brilliance. Another editor reads it, and she wants you to write something similar for her. The invoice is paid on time. You meet someone for lunch. Or you write a piece. Strangers tell you they hate it. Your editor ignores your chipper emails. You pitch to another editor: she ignores you too. The invoice never gets processed, and your friend cancels on your lunch.

You might say that every workday is like this. But at ordinary workplaces, you have colleagues, a schedule, a reliable pay cheque. In the world of the freelancer, there is no one to complain to, or sympathize with, and no one to catch you when there's nothing between you and the world's opinion of you.

I WANT A DOG
"I want a dog," I told him.

Some people want a dog for companionship, and some people want a dog as a jogging buddy. I was asking for one thing from my dog: consistency. "I want something that feels the same way about me every day," I said.

I wanted the love on the good days to be the exact same quality and quantity as the love on the bad days. We talk a lot about unconditional love, but we don't speak enough about unconditional like. My family loves me always, but they don't like me the same amount every day. My partner loves me always, but his opinion of me day-to-day can fluctuate, depending on whether I have cleaned the egg pan or not. Love is the immovable bedrock at the centre of any meaningful relationship: like is the topsoil just above it, forever being scooped and swept and heaped and smashed. If all we needed in this life was unconditional love, then the phrase "you know I love you unconditionally" wouldn't so commonly be followed by "but, here's some incredibly precise, accurate and inadvertently hurtful feedback".

" "

YOU NEED
BOREDOM
AND ROUTINE
AND SOMEONE
TO MUTELY SIT
THERE AND TELL
YOU YOU'RE
DOING FINE

The dog does not have feedback. The dog thinks I'm cool regardless of what I do. I cannot stress enough how much my dog thinks I'm the coolest person on earth. If I write a piece that 50,000 people read, my dog thinks I'm great. If I don't get out of bed until noon, and I eat cornflake cakes for breakfast and I say something bitchy about someone I'm jealous of, my dog thinks I'm great.

She's got this way of listening when I talk to her – you probably know it, if you have a dog. She has one ear up, one ear down, a little twitch in the side of her mouth and her paws are crossed together. The whole expression comes together as, "Yes, you were saying? Go on?"

The long-term health benefits of having a pet are plentiful and obvious. Even petting an animal with fur for a short time has been proven to reduce anxiety. But as hard as I look, I can't seem to find a study that proves that your dog's utter faith in your humanity will make you feel like more of a human, every day.

TIME PASSES

Days turn into weeks, weeks into months. The novelty of a puppy wears off and she learns, eventually, that she cannot command my attention all the time. She begins to respect my deadlines, and waits patiently for when I take her out, after lunch. Except, no. That never happens. Not even a little.

She is not the only dog around. There are other freelancers, other dogs, other people who are gazing into their pets' eyes, freely using walks and vet visits as valid excuses not to get any work done. In the area I live in, Sylvie does not rank highly when it comes to glamour. She's not graceful, like the herds of whippets and Italian greyhounds that career around the edge of the dog park. She's not intellectual, like the slow-blinking French bulldogs that stare her down when she enters cafés. She's not stop-what-you're-doing cute, like the pugs, dachshunds, and labradoodles that regularly stop traffic in my area. Our daily walk is exactly an hour and 20 minutes long, and goes through some of the richest and poorest boroughs of London. We start in Deptford, where I have to tug her away from eating discarded fish bones from the street market. We cross a Catholic churchyard (eerily similar to the kind of church I attended as a child in Ireland) and come through to London's leafy Greenwich. We journey through the park, me heaving to keep up with her, climbing the mud-slipped hill to the onion-shaped observatory until I'm winded.

We cross to Blackheath. Children in immaculate sports kits swarm around Sylvie, and beg to give her a treat. We stop for a few minutes, and walk on. Well, I walk: she bounds forward. Minutes later, we're crossing through New Cross, where children shrink their bodies against the wall in order to avoid Sylvie's wet, inquiring nose. They shriek when she comes near them, and their mothers – exhausted, overprotective, weighed down with shopping bags and not enough time – tell them to stay away from "that dog". I used to be offended. "She's really friendly," I would say, until I realized that it made no difference how friendly Sylvie was. Some people grow up in a context where dogs are used to frighten and intimidate. Some children walk to school alone, past gates where unhappy dogs bark at them. Not everyone gets a clean sports kit, or a clean slate. Our daily walk proves that to me, over time.

That's not something I can change. *Nor is it something I'm responsible for.*

"THE DOG THINKS I'M COOL REGARDLESS OF WHAT I DO. I CANNOT STRESS ENOUGH HOW MUCH MY DOG THINKS I'M THE COOLEST PERSON ON EARTH"

We complete our circuit of south-east London. Rich areas, poor areas, in-between areas: it's just the two of us, noses to the air. Sylvie continues to be extra. She wants love, she wants attention, she wants to go see what outside smells like today. She *has* to know what the inside of my mouth smells like, emails be damned. There is no point reasoning with her that I have people to please and invoices to chase: to her, a new war starts every day, and that war starts with getting me out of my chair so I will play with her. Again, it doesn't matter how polite I'm being. It doesn't matter if I have smacked her on the bum gently for being too much of a handful. Same Caroline; same war; same smells. Different day.

SYLVIE AND CAROLINE

A NOTE ON SMELLS

A note on smells: because of the way a dog's nose is configured, they use smell to tell the time in the same way we use light.

"A strong odor is probably a newer odor, laid down more recently," says writer Alexandra Horowitz.

......

A weaker odor is something that was left in the past. So in being able to detect the concentration of a smell, they're really seeing not only what it is but how long ago it was left. So when being able to detect the concentration of a smell, they're really seeing not only what it is, but how long ago it was left. So the past, for instance, when you walk outside your door is underfoot, who's walked by, what, you know, skin have they sloughed, leaving some evidence of their voyage, what animals have passed by? And the future, in a way, is smelled on a breeze from up ahead or around a corner.

So I feel like time is rubber-banded for dogs through smell. And it also allows them to detect things which we don't think are really visible yet, like dogs often are said to be able to detect an upcoming storm.

......

I think about this a lot. The immediate past as a series of old smells, like rotting leaves or put-out fires. The immediate future: just stick your nose in it, go find out, it's right here, right in this grass, right in this bin, right in this person's mouth! I start interpreting my dog's attempts to leap inside me as something else: in her own way, she thinks she's saving me. "Why are you still back there, with all those old thoughts and day-old worries? Come out! Come out!"

She is coaxing me out of myself, luring me into being extra with her. "You're like me," she says. "You're a little much. *We* are a little much."

"Don't you see that people hate it, though?" I reply. "Don't you understand that the whippet over there, the one you're so intent on being friends with, is actually furious that you're jumping all over him, and getting mud on his fancy posh coat?"

"Well, if he *will* wear white to the dog park."

"You're not funny."

"Au contraire: I am hugely funny. Everyone thinks so. Even you think so. Look, I'm going to jump inside your face again, so I can have a chat with the idiot who is running things in there."

"You're terrible."

"No, I'm not. I'm the exact same dog that I was yesterday. And the day before, and the day before."

So here's the thing I finally understood about midway through my 300th imaginary conversation with my own dog: she thinks I am the same every day because I *am* the same every day.

35

It seems obvious, but in reality, it was the root of all my problems: my sleeplessness, the anxious knot in my stomach, the terror at every email I received – I kidded myself into believing that because people's reactions to me changed every day, that I changed also. If an editor or a reader didn't like my work on Tuesday, but did on Wednesday, it made no difference to who I was: I was the exact same bag of bones on both days, no better or worse.

I've met adults who shrink away from my dog, but equally, have seen three-year-old children treat her like something between a sibling and a tiny horse. She can't control how people are going to react to her, but she can control how she reacts to them. I think about all the writers, artists, designers and actors I know whose work would be infinitely better if they made the simple realization that my dog was somehow born with: that you cannot control how people feel about you. That you can care about people, while simultaneously ignoring what they think.

I finished my first book. I started my second. I am now mere days from finishing it, a job I do in-between walking my dog and explaining patiently to her that I cannot walk her yet. It seems amazing to me that while I was introducing this mad little animal to half of London, work was also happening. Simultaneously, I grew a puppy into a dog, and a collection of ideas into a novel. I noticed that the bigger Sylvie got, the more regular my heartbeat became. Days became consistent, patterned, routine-driven. My sleep improved. I let go of the idea that in order to create great work, I had to live in a garret, drinking myself to oblivion, while wearing one half of a single pair of pyjamas shared with the painter next door. I learned that being creative and being bohemian were entirely separate things, and that for most writers, chaos is not a prerequisite. You need boredom and routine, and someone to mutely sit there and tell you you're doing fine. Someone to pull you out of yourself, through the mouth, if necessary.

It shouldn't have taken a white-haired, pop-eyed, extra-as-hell Jack Russell to teach me to like myself a little more, but it did. And now, regardless of the day, or the editor, or the article I'm writing, I try to keep that sense of self-forgiveness close by. I like you, I say to her, and she does her "Yes, go on?" face again. "And I like myself," I continue. "Unconditionally."

PAWS FOR THOUGHT

Being kinder to yourself

1 | FEEDBACK

You don't worry about what your dog thinks of you, yet you like one another unconditionally. You trust that whatever you do, your dog will forgive you. Treat yourself with the same respect.

2 | ONLY YOU

Once you accept that people don't have to like your dog, you realize they don't have to like anything about you either. Substitute "dog" for "hair", "cooking" or "novel".

3 | LIKE YOURSELF

It's easy to like yourself when life is exciting. It's harder when it's just you, your body and a long trudge walk. If you can like yourself when you're bored with yourself, you're doing good.

4 | BE FORGIVING

The first day I got her, my dog pooped worms on the rug. I thought I'd never forgive her. But I did. If you can forgive your dog for being born with worms, you can forgive yourself a number of things.

5 | WALK…

Walk. Drink water. Eat three times a day. This is enough to keep your dog happy. If you are feeling anxious or scared, ask yourself: When did I last walk? When did I last drink water? When did I last eat? It won't fix everything, but it's a damned fine start.

CHAPTER 3

TIME MAKERS AND MINDFUL OBSERVERS

TIME MAKERS AND
MINDFUL OBSERVERS

Living in the moment with cats for company

Clare Barry | Urban Curiosity

My friend Susannah believes cats can help us to slow down and reclaim time for what really matters. Felines have a different timetable, she tells me. And they provide a punctuation point in their owners' day. I'm not crazy about felines (please don't hold it against me if you are), but witnessing Susannah's happiness since a local cat sauntered through the open bathroom window in her home, I've been giving this some thought.

Like me, Susannah is a writer and online business owner. We find it easy to spend too much time on our laptops working or indulging in Netflix binges; being single and living alone means we can suit ourselves. We've also both suffered with grief: in 2005, Susannah's partner died very suddenly from a heart attack; a decade later, my mother passed away after a short, unexpected illness. We both know from hard experience how horrible insomnia is and what a negative impact it has on our happiness and mental resilience; grief can distort time and steal our sleep, while depression affects more than 300 million people worldwide, according to the United Nations. How can animals make us feel less stressed and more peaceful?

CREATE PAUSES

In autumn 2017, the cat appeared in Susannah's house each day. She fell in love with her green eyes and white coat with splodges of black and orange. After asking around, she discovered the pussy had turned up in the local pub some

" "

TIME, ENERGY AND
ATTENTION ARE,
PERHAPS, OUR
MOST PRECIOUS
RESOURCES;
OFTEN, WE SPEND
THEM FREELY ON
EXPERIENCES AND
WORRIES THAT, IN
THE END, DON'T
MATTER SO MUCH

time earlier, but didn't really belong to anyone. An amicable conversation with the landlord followed and today, Cat, as Susannah calls her new housemate, forces her to create pauses in the day. I confess to feeling a little jealous.

"SHE'S CHILLED ME OUT BY LYING ON ME QUITE HEAVILY!"

"She's chilled me out by lying on me quite heavily!" laughs Susannah. "I'm a first-time cat servant; if she was a kitten, it would be different, but because she's older, she likes to just lie on me. She's very much a lap-cat. When that happens, I might be able to look at my phone a bit, but I can't work. I don't even read. I'm less interested in television and it's because of her. I turn the sound down because it bothers Cat. She lies here and I stroke her and I get a bit snoozy. It's been so nice to have a quiet evening."

42

EXPLORE WHAT MATTERS

Time, energy and attention are, perhaps, our most precious resources; often, we spend them freely on experiences and worries that, in the end, don't matter so much. We scroll through social-media feeds and struggle with comparison or feel anxious about news headlines. We strive for the ideal partner, job or home; the right type of holidays, hobbies and purchases. We ruminate and ponder.

Animals can help us examine our true priorities and get into the here and now. "Cat demands one-to-one attention," says Susannah. She insists on full engagement and even sits on her owner's keyboard if necessary. "I'm trying to get my work done in the morning now because I know she'll pad down in the afternoon and want to be in my lap and I'll give in, so it's the end of working. She's caused me to focus differently."

This really captures my interest. I am a champion procrastinator (or would be if there were such a prize). For example, I have missed my deadline for submitting this chapter. As 5pm approached, I found myself in the kitchen cooking a chicken-and-mushroom pie for my pal next door and baking almond chocolate

Chapter 3 | TIME MAKERS AND MINDFUL OBSERVERS

cakes. It has taken my writing avoidance to another level. I've had all week to write and somehow the time has slipped away, as I focused on other projects and priorities that were not as important to me as this commission. If I had my own pet, perhaps I would choose to do things differently in order to enjoy hanging out with it. Would owning a kitty have helped me hit my deadline?

I always procrastinate, but lately I've been emotionally wobbly too. On a bad day, my mind fizzes with thoughts and my body floods with adrenalin when a panic attack strikes. The idea of a pet to help calm my system and give me something different to concentrate on is very appealing. "Cat is company and that's lovely, especially when you're single. It's not that she gives me love, but that I can give her love," explains Susannah. "That brings a sense of purpose. Me looking after her and making sure she's OK takes the focus off me, which is really good."

In *The Tao of Meow*, Deborah Wood writes about her pet:

......

[She] *understands the primal, natural ways of the world. She leaps into the air, ethereal as sunlight, and connects to the energy of the sky. She relaxes her body so profoundly that she becomes heavy to lift, rooted to the energy of the earth. She is loving yet independent, wiry yet soft, ferocious yet friendly. A cat is the ultimate Taoist. The epitome of yin-yang, the cat is perfectly balanced between tame and wild, sociability and solitude, action and rest.*

......

UNOFFICIAL MEDITATION
Despite my reticence to welcome a four-legged animal into my home, I'm tuning into the ways felines can teach us to focus and observe. Have you ever watched a pet await a treat? My brother and his partner have two cats: O'Malley, a domestic shorthair, and Oliver, a ginger. Each one's entire being – the intensity of its gaze, the tilt of its head, its stillness – is aimed at my brother's hand as he offers up that small item of delight. After his snack,

" "

PERHAPS OUR
FELINE FRIENDS CAN
TEACH US HUMANS A
THING OR TWO ABOUT
BEING MINDFUL AND
TRULY PRESENT WITH
EACH OTHER

Oliver will recline on the sofa and gaze at my brother as if to say: "Here I am. Love me, need me, want me." The cat is exposed and totally vulnerable in that moment. Perhaps our feline friends can teach us humans a thing or two about being mindful and truly present with each other.

Cats can even help us make time for meditation. Susannah's morning routine since Cat arrived in her house is a meditative one. "If I sit on the bathroom floor in the morning, and she's in my lap, then I'll just sit there and close my eyes sometimes for up to 30 minutes. She's encouraging me to slow down more. Animals live in the moment and she's helping me to just be there in the moment: whether that's sitting still or having a cuddle."

Space to think or just be is powerful. My meditation practice becomes hardest in the times when I need it most because my busy mind is full of mental chatter and trivial worries. I welcome any kind of interruption from this noise. A cat plonking itself on my lap would be a break from this, and the idea of being physically rooted to the spot thanks to someone else – albeit a whiskered creature – is tempting. Then I think about my existing rationale to remain pet-free: I travel abroad often. I don't like cat hair all over my clothes. I don't particularly enjoy touching them and I really don't like handling cat food (I've fed neighbours' cats over the years). Susannah tries to convince me to get a pussy and I resist. I reach for my smartphone instead.

CAT VIDEOS ARE A FORM OF THERAPY

I'm no feline fan and yet I find myself howling at the skittishness of a kitten with a cardboard tube or the grey kitten perched on the shell of a moving tortoise. It can be therapeutic, joyful even, to see these clips. My nieces and I swap links and text each other emoticon-filled messages of delight. The animals show us acrobatic feats, make us wonder at their agility and laugh at their intent. They provoke an emotional reaction and, in my family, they help us bond across the generations.

My eldest niece is doing her GCSEs. When she is feeling stressed out by her studies she opens up YouTube and types "cat videos" in the search box. It returns 95 million results! A few clips later and she swears she feels better.

In 2015, a preliminary study by Jessica Gall Myrick, a media scholar at Indiana University, USA, suggested cat videos provoke positive emotions in humans and reduce negative ones. This is unsurprising given the research around the constructive impact of pet therapy on individuals with behavioural or medical difficulties and on their emotional wellbeing in general. When it comes to cat videos, it may not be the case that they're trivial or a waste of time. We watch them because we like how they make us feel. And they provide social glue: my nieces and I are typical in being fully engaged in this type of media. We comment on and share these types of cute or funny clips, whereas other Internet consumption tends to be more passive.

"IT'S SO NICE TO HAVE ANOTHER HEARTBEAT IN THE HOUSE AND ANOTHER PAIR OF EYES."

And it's not just YouTube where cats rule the world. The website LolCats allows users to share pictures of their cats and the team transforms them into LOLCat memes – pictures with amusing or touching captions. The site gets more than 100 million views per month. Over on Instagram, there's Choupette Lagerfeld (pampered kitty of fashion designer Karl) with 109,000 followers, and Smoothie the Cat, aka the "Queen of Fluff", with 1.3 million. I find Grumpy Cat's feed hilarious, and 2.4 million followers seem to agree. There's endless reach. These images can provide a little mental refreshment in a hectic day. Perhaps virtual time with cats is as much exposure to them as I need in order to lift my spirits on difficult days.

WALK ON THE WILD SIDE

Of course, cats have a natural predatory instinct, which explains why the average domestic kitty may proudly present its owner with a mangled rodent at breakfast time or enjoy tormenting feathery creatures, despite being well fed and watered. In some ways, cats give us a licence to accept our own wildness. They like to roam and prowl. Watching those vignettes online shows me how cats allow and like us to misbehave – just as they do. They encourage us to get

SUSANNAH'S CAT

silly and to leave the seriousness of modern life behind us for a few moments by playing with them. "Cat has a moment twice a day when she likes to play attack. A frenetic energy that just bursts out," says Susannah. "It's really cute when she does it. And as a newbie cat servant, I've learned that you simply have to go with their natural ways of being. You can't really train them; they do whatever they want."

"CAT VIDEOS PROVOKE POSITIVE EMOTIONS IN HUMANS AND REDUCE NEGATIVE ONES"

I see this with my brother's cats. If he wants to pet them and it doesn't suit them, they ignore him or wriggle out of his embrace. When they want to delight in his attention, they stop at nothing until he responds. O'Malley will rub up against my brother's ankle or sit on his feet when he wants to be petted. He purrs with contentment at having his fur stroked, while Oliver rolls onto his back and waits for his pale belly to be rubbed. They have the easy ability to receive affection which, many of us humans lack.

The idea of dancing like no one's watching isn't new, but how often do we adults truly let ourselves go and enjoy how we feel, rather than worry about how we'll be perceived? The way cats indulge their desires and wild side is something I vow to remember as I go through my days and work toward feeling more peaceful and calm. I've spent the first half of my life striving to fit social norms. Throw in my own unrealistic expectations, perfectionism and some grief, and it's no wonder I feel flat. I may not be a cat person, but perhaps I can become more cat-like in my approach to life. They like to sleep a lot and sleep is healing. Bed feels like a good place to start!

REDUCE STRESS AND EASE DEPRESSION AT A CAT CAFÉ

Recently, my doctor prescribed me antidepressants. I didn't want to take them at first, though now I accept I've been low for a long time – even before this more recent grief that has compounded everything. "When I'm feeling down,

I nip upstairs and we have a cuddle on the bed and it always brightens up my mood," says Susannah. "It's so nice to have another heartbeat in the house and another pair of eyes."

Studies have found cats help to alleviate depression and stress because their presence and touch can release the stress-reducing and immune-boosting chemicals dopamine and serotonin in us. Susannah is proof of this – she's chilled out, content and healthy. This is why I agree to visit Lady Dinah's Cat Emporium in London's East End.

Cat cafés originated in Japan and Taiwan; now they're everywhere. They appeal to people who cannot have cats for health or lifestyle reasons, who may have lost a beloved pet or who are curious about "cat therapy" and the soothing effect these furry beings can have on humans. A brief poke around the Internet assures me these establishments have the animals' welfare as a priority.

Susannah and I head in the direction of the Emporium, named after the feline character in *Alice in Wonderland*. This venue – like other kitty cafés – is really popular and it's taken us days to get a reservation for the High Tea with Cats slot. I am not sure what to expect as I step inside.

There is a pair of tortoiseshell moggies lounging in the corner and a ginger elongates its torso in a lovely stretch. The crowd is a mixture of tourists and hipsters. Everyone seems thrilled to be there. We settle down and hardly say a word to each other. Susannah coos over a tabby and I study the room.

These cats bring their whole self to just one thing, whether that's sleeping, cuddling, playing or eating. We humans value multi-tasking and are often disconnected from our inner wisdom. Cats do one thing at a time; they are connected to their inner needs. They teach us to honour our instincts. They seek out rest, sustenance, affection, play, a good stretch or simply to be left alone, and they are single-minded about getting what they want. In the past, I didn't honour my instincts and often suffered for it. My intuition or gut feeling about people and situations was often right, but the people-pleaser in me shut it down.

Today, I try to do what's best for me.

This mode of being can be applied to human existence, if only we would make space to slow down long enough to listen to what we need and act upon it.

A couple of hours later, I emerge from the wacky place. I walk along the street and make my confession to Susannah: I simply don't like cats. I understand how they are a source of joy and peace to many people, but I find it hard to connect with them.

In the process of writing this chapter, however, all the kitty-related focus has taught me, or at least reminded me, of the importance of getting proper rest, the joy of naps, why honouring my instinct matters and that asking for attention or affection is totally acceptable. These steps may well help me as I move toward a brighter future and reduce my antidepressants with my GP's help. While I may not enjoy hanging out with them, I am grateful to these four-legged animals for the lessons and reminders they offer.

50

Cats can help us pursue a less stressful and more peaceful life, which is the key to thriving in a hyper-connected and fast-paced world. They are the ultimate time makers and mindful observers.

I am grateful to these feline teachers who truly live in each moment.

PAWS FOR THOUGHT

Feline mindful living

1 | FELINE PACE
We race through our days and often miss out on ordinary moments of beauty or delight. Slow down, find a warm spot to curl up and watch the world pass by.

2 | PUT PEOPLE ON TOP
We often yearn for more time to do the things we love and to hang out with the people that we cherish. Challenge yourself to see if your priorities could push the people you love higher up the list.

3 | CAT PAWS
Perhaps you don't have a large cat to interrupt you, forcing a pause through a little gentle squashing. However, taking a regular moment out to do something as relaxing as stroking soft, warm fur makes for a worthwhile recharge.

4 | FELINE WISDOM
When you next feel overwhelmed by the stuff you need to do and the little time you have available, take a moment to watch the movements of a feline friend. Cats are time makers and observers; they can help us live a mindful life.

CHAPTER 4

DAILY WONDER

CHAPTER 4

DAILY WONDER

Discovering the world through canine eyes

Rabbi Jonathan Wittenberg | Author of *Things My Dog Has Taught Me: About being a better human*

The sky was brightening across the steep valley, which fell away below. The birds sang as they swooped toward their nests beneath the eaves. But it wasn't their music which had woken us. It was our young dog, Mitzpah; he'd forced us out of bed, in uniquely puppy style, by messing all across the floor.

Nicky, my wife, and I cleaned up his delightful deposits, then looked at one other. It wasn't exactly our custom to go for a walk at four in the morning, but the May dawn light was simply too enticing. We took Mitzpah by the collar, let our fourteen-year-old dog, Safi, snooze on undisturbed and set off into the emerging day.

Mitzpah was delighted; it was farming country, so we didn't dare let him run free, but he tugged and danced at the end of his lead. On either side of the woodland paths the last of the bluebells bloomed in drifts beneath the oaks. The lambs bleated sharply from the valley floor, soothed by the calming calls of the ewes. When we reached the paddock next to the farmhouse, an intrepid sheep stretched its neck through a gap in the fence and Mitzpah, a Welsh Border collie, had his first close encounter with the breed he was born to herd. For a moment, he and the sheep touched noses, then enthusiasm overwhelmed him – he barked and the sheep backed swiftly away to join her comrades in their field.

Meanwhile, the sun had begun to warm the crisp late-spring air and the blackbirds, the thrushes, the tits and the finches all sang. "Listen," said Nicky, touching my arm: from high in the hillside came the call of a cuckoo.

54

" "

I THINK OF HOW
MUCH MORE DETAIL
I HAVE NOTICED –
A GNARLED TREE BOW
OR TWILIGHT THRUSHES
– BECAUSE THE DOG
HAS BEEN MY GUIDE

All the way back up the lane, the trees entranced us: the yellow-green of the younger leaves still unfurling from the cusp of their buds, the deep, shining green of the more mature foliage, caught in the morning brightness. "Glory be to God for dappled things": it must have been in a place like this that the great British poet Gerard Manley Hopkins was inspired to write those words.

Mitzpah paid more attention to the roots and grasses, his eager snout guiding him from tuft to tuft and twig to twig, his outsized ears erect, his gait and gaze all zestful energy. He tugged us up the hill, then back a few paces to further savour the whiff of some story encapsulated in p-mails (a charming expression that refers to how dogs read the scents of other dogs from their pee). For once pressure-free, with no urgent demands ticking away in our brains, we let him set the pace.

Safi raised his head gently when we returned, as if to say, "Thank you for letting me sleep". Mitzpah settled down beside him, and we too curled up with our dreams.

Twelve years on, Nicky and I still draw joy from the glory of that morning. "It was all your fault," I say, stroking the ears of a now much older, but no less eager, animal. Whenever I say the Jewish daily prayer, "I give thanks to you, God, for returning me to life", I give thanks too for the companionship of that dog; and when I come to the words "How wonderful are your works", I think of how much more detail I have noticed – a gnarled tree bow or twilight thrushes – because the dog has been my guide.

DISCOVERING TRANSPORT

To see the world through the nose and paws of a dog is different from perceiving it through human eyes.

Take transport, for instance. Safi, our first dog, black and medium-sized, a mixture of a Staffordshire bull terrier and a Labrador with maybe a few collie genes, used to sing in the car. It wouldn't have made the charts; there was little that was musical about it, at least to the non-canine ear. But if songs are about joy and enthusiasm, then it certainly fitted the definition. As soon as we turned off the "M" and the "A" roads, as soon as trees and fields could be seen through the windows and the fragrance of park or countryside began to displace the stuffy air inside the car, Safi would sit up on the back seat and whine, growl and yelp with eager delight. Mitzpah, too, has always loved the car, clambering eagerly onto the back seat at the first opportunity, even if he knows he will inevitably get no further than the underground car park at the supermarket, but hopeful, always, that he will end up at some outdoor haven.

Unlike Safi, Mitzpah also loves the London Underground. It was there that he almost cost me my career. It happened during the rush hour, when I was foolish enough to take him in the hope that it would accustom him to crowds. The carriage was crammed with passengers and I found myself squeezed in next to a young and rather pretty woman, who suddenly said loudly, "Who just touched my arse?" Silence descended and there was a distinct sense of awkwardness, when the culprit turned and licked his victim's hand. Happily, the woman burst out laughing and patted Mitzpah on the head.

"I WISH I KNEW HOW TO MAKE PEOPLE SMILE IN THE WAY THAT HE DOES"

A far more exciting experience for him is the overground train, especially the overnight sleeper. I think Mitzpah even knows when our Underground train pulls in at the overground station. I can feel the excitement in his body as I carry him up the escalator. Mercifully, he doesn't wriggle, but places his front paw around my neck and makes cute faces at passing commuters. I wish I knew how to make people smile in the way that he does. He takes advantage of every lamppost as we walk along the platform looking for our carriage, and once inside, he either crawls under or – if he's feeling bold – onto the bottom bunk, to dream blissful dreams of forests, mountain streams and the fragments of scone which will fall (accidentally, of course) from the tables of dog-friendly Scottish cafés.

" "

DOG OWNERSHIP
OFFERS THE CHANCE
TO RE-EXPERIENCE IT
THROUGH THE NOSE,
TONGUE, EARS AND
PAWS OF ONE'S DOG

DISCOVERING THE ELEMENTS

More exhilarating by far, however, has been to witness our dogs' first encounters with previously unfamiliar features of the natural world. While parenthood provides the moving opportunity to rediscover the world's magic through the eyes of one's children, dog ownership offers the chance to re-experience it through the nose, tongue, ears and paws of one's dog.

Safi's been gone now for more than 11 years and nostalgic memories are tinged with sorrow. I recall like yesterday the first time he came across the sea. He raced toward the water's edge and, before we could stop him, lowered his head for a long, deep drink. The look on his face when he found out the water was salty was a unique mixture of shock and rebuke: "Why didn't you warn me?" he seemed to be saying as he shook his head in disgust.

When Safi first saw snow, from the steps of the overnight train, he refused to alight onto the strange white powder which had obliterated the platform. Only when I descended ahead of him would he gingerly place his paws on the fronts of my shoes, before daring to take a tentative, hesitant step on his own. I remember, too, Mitzpah's first experiences on ice: all four of his paws gave way in different directions, leaving him doing the quadruple splits.

Rivers, however, were no problem for Safi. From the outset, he would plunge enthusiastically into the water, dive for the biggest pebbles and deposit them on the bank. Then he would climb out and shake himself off as near to us as possible, under the pretence that no, of course he hadn't intended to get us all soaked. Mitzpah, in contrast, drew back when he first saw a stream. Safi tried to persuade him: "Go on," he seemed to be saying to his recalcitrant young acolyte, with a nudge of his nose. And it was a while before it worked, but now Mitzpah is as eager a paddler, and no less addicted to the water and the waves.

Mercifully, Safi never managed to transmit to Mitzpah his perverse love of ropes. As soon as he saw one suspended from a branch he would break into a run, jump up, hang on with his teeth and swing back and forth. His legs would be wobbling like an inebriated rock-and-roller's, and all the while he'd be emitting an uninterrupted concerto of yowls and howls which had the embarrassing effect of attracting everyone around to witness the display.

Getting him down involved prising open his jaws, while holding tightly to his collar; otherwise, he'd be back up and dancing in no time.

THE WONDER AND THE LOVE

Dogs sometimes do get depressed, when their human partner goes away without them, when they lose a companion or when they grow old and can no longer undertake the adventures they once used to relish. But far more often, they take life on the nose, as it comes, with eagerness and affection.

"I FEEL AS IF I'VE BEEN PERMITTED A GLIMPSE INTO THE WONDER AT THE VERY HEART OF LIFE, LED THERE BY MY DOG"

My dogs have brought magic back into my everyday workaholic world and they've done it not once, but over and over again. They have also initiated me into new mysteries in life.

I would never go out so often close to midnight if Mitzpah didn't chide me by the door with his body language, as though saying: "What? Are you really going to go to bed without our late-night walk? Are you truly going to make me miss the midnight scents?" It's no use pretending to a dog that tomorrow is another day. So, yielding with only minimal weary resentment, I take him to our local green space, where we hear owls calling from the great oaks, see bats flying in rapid zigzags across the edge of the pond and listen to the silent breathing of the trees.

Sometimes, in the forest, we come upon a herd of deer, and I hold his collar before he has the chance to race off after them. Or a single hind crosses our shadowed path, pausing for a moment to stare at us, before springing back into the trees. Then, because I love deer, and because the fleeting witnessing of their presence seems such a privilege, I feel as if I've been permitted a glimpse into the wonder at the very heart of life, led there by my dog.

And sometimes, back in London, we see a baby hedgehog, curled tight in alarm at our sudden proximity. Mitzpah sniffs, while I stare down at the small, precious ball of a creature which has so far evaded cars and foxes. Then I draw the dog away from the frightened animal and watch from a distance. I see it slowly unfurl, revealing its tiny snout, and its little legs re-emerging from underneath its prickles. Now and then, it takes itself off with unexpected speed toward the privacy of the thick grass and the nettles entangled in the bramble thicket. And I recall Thomas Hardy's sad poem:

.....

If I pass during some nocturnal blackness, mothy and warm,

When the hedgehog travels furtively over the lawn,

One may say, "He strove that such innocent creatures should come to no harm...

But he could do little for them; and now he is gone."

.....

At such moments, my heart fills with a love that connects me to all the living beings around me – the night birds, the hedgehogs and even the trees. The Jewish mystics speak of the sphere of loving kindness, one of the ten vital qualities of the eternal energy that flows through all creation. It fills both Mitzpah's consciousness and mine, uniting us in the sacred bond of life. For a few precious seconds, awareness holds me still in silent wonder. I look up and see the few stars London's light pollution leaves free for us to stare at on clear nights, while the half-moon briefly vanishes, occluded by the wind-driven flight of a band of tattered cloud. Released for these few moments from the burden of thoughts, which so frequently beset me and complicate my mind, I experience pure, happy, simple, unselfconscious being.

Then Mitzpah runs back and looks up at me impatiently, as if to say: "You, lazybones, can't you be bothered to walk a little further?" and we resume our night-time pilgrimage.

MITZPAH AND JONATHAN

WICKED MOMENTS

It would be wrong to give the false impression that where my dogs are concerned, everything is always perfect, pious innocence.

"Look," said my daughter some years ago, as we were completing a long day's walking in the Scottish Highlands. She pointed toward the river beside which our path, now mercifully level and easy, ran.

"Yes," I said, staring at the rocks and trees that lined the water's edge.

"More carefully," she insisted.

I took note of three sheep swimming downstream at remarkable speed. "Sheep," I replied naively.

"And again," she said.

It was only then that I noticed Mitzpah doing a rapid canine breaststroke close behind them. Mercifully, just as I began to yell at him, all four creatures clambered safely onto the bank.

This reminded me of when Nicky was pregnant with our first child and we took a last short break à deux (or two humans and one canine) in the Scottish Highlands. We were walking down a steep, stony track when we overtook some women whose attention had been grabbed by a scene below. Beneath was a wide, shallow river divided by a small island onto which two sheep were scrambling, chased by a dark shadow with an embarrassingly familiar shape. "I wonder whose dog that could be?" one of them said. Nicky and I walked swiftly past, then broke into a downhill run, shouting and gesticulating as we went.

Nothing was quite as embarrassing, however, as the sunny spring afternoon, when a family of hikers decided to unpack their picnic at the precise point where two paths met in the middle of a large open space. Mitzpah, who never liked to be behind us, got there first. I couldn't blame him for concluding that the sandwiches had been laid out specially for his delectation. And I was impressed – and relieved – that he only helped himself to one (perhaps the mayonnaise wasn't to his taste). Before I could apologise, the family, who took the whole affair in good humour, acknowledged that perhaps it hadn't been the wisest location in which to spread out their lunch.

These are the minor misdemeanours of which I'm aware; no doubt there are plenty more that I don't even know about.

WATER, ROCK AND AWE

Most challenging of all are the long adventures Mitzpah and I have undertaken among the lakes and mountains of the far north of Scotland, Britain's final wilderness. Sometimes, one of the children has accompanied us; more often, we've set out just he and I among the heather and the hills. The path ascends and simply vanishes above the outcrops of rock, which fall almost vertically into the water, many feet below. We take our bearings from the direction of the lake, following from high above it the line of the water from west to east. Below us, for a while, lies a steep, dense remnant of ancient forest.

65

> "WE'RE TOGETHER ON THIS EARTH,
> YOU AND I…I LOVE YOU," I SAID.
> "AND WITHOUT LOVE WE'RE HELPLESS"

Once, I got lost within it and struggled to progress, fearful of the pits and caverns beneath the slippery moss-covered trunks and the dead branches, too rotten to trust. Mitzpah slid and slithered, more lithe than me, till we made our merciful exit back out onto the open space. Then the contours forced us to climb, aiming for a gap between two peaks, the gateway into another pass below the mountains, above another lake. All day we met no humans; for hours, no other living being, save insects and the small birds flying anxiously up among the long grasses and the reeds.

When eventually we did emerge among some sheep, and then into a field of horses, I greeted my fellow beings with heartfelt joy, glad of their companionship on earth.

But the greatest companion was Mitzpah. Without him, I'm not sure I would have dared to undertake this experience – albeit brief and limited – of smallness and vulnerability among the rocks and water and sky. Present just as they had been since the Ice Age, they chastened me; and touched by awe and fear, I recognized the brief measure of my mortality. I bent down to stroke Mitzpah's head and, reassured by the feel of his faithful companionship, I told him: "But we're together on this earth, you and I...I love you," I said. "And without love we're helpless, both you and I."

Mitzpah looked up at me for a moment, and I didn't know if he was offering me an affectionate, don't-get-the-words-but-do-get-the-feeling "Yes'", or if he was just anxious to be back on the trail.

"Humankind cannot bear very much reality,' wrote T S Eliot. But with a dog by one's side one can bear more.

When we got back to our cottage, I fed Mitzpah, dried him down with his towel and he climbed onto our bed where, making sure he took up sufficient room to prevent me and Nicky from joining him, he slept the untroubled sleep of the righteous. Only now and then his paws moved back and forth, as if he'd just heard the magic word "Walk" and was accelerating from an amble into a run.

PAWS FOR THOUGHT

Six Canine Commandments

1 | SAY YES TO LIFE
It will say yes back.

2 | EXPLORE THE WORLD
Begin on your doorstep.

3 | FIND WONDER
You don't have to go far.

4 | KEEP EARS AND EYES SHARP
Wellsprings of joy and compassion are all around us.

5 | BE LOVING
Hopefully others will be loving to you, too.

6 | SEIZE THE DAY
Especially dawn and twilight.

CHAPTER 5

BOUNCING BACK

CHAPTER 5

BOUNCING BACK

How to deal with life's knocks

Kate Peers | Author of the blog *Mad about the boys*

My life was fairly straightforward until my mid-20s. I worked as an account manager in a top advertising agency, making TV ads and creating award-winning campaigns. We partied hard, entertained clients at the top restaurants and enjoyed the huge expense accounts, living the *Mad Men* reality. It was a dream job for someone just a year out of university.

Then came the big crash and I was in the first of several rounds of redundancies. My ego took a big blow; I took a huge knock. Nothing had ever really gone wrong in my life before. This was a first.

With no jobs at all in the industry, I had to ride out the recession. Jobs in general were scarce and the competition fierce. Interviews comprised four rounds – I would get to the final one or two and then the other person would be picked. It was hard to keep up morale, but I did, and after 31 interviews I finally got back into advertising.

At the time, I didn't think about it much. I was too busy back working and playing hard. But now, when I look back, I'm surprised at how I managed to keep going when I was continually being knocked back. Where did I learn the skills to be so resilient – to pick myself up, put my best foot forward and go forth smiling into the next round of interviews?

I realize that I had seen lessons in resilience at home, and often they came in the form of the four-legged creatures I grew up with. But how, you might ask. Bear with me, we will get there in a little while.

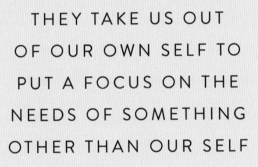

" "

THEY TAKE US OUT
OF OUR OWN SELF TO
PUT A FOCUS ON THE
NEEDS OF SOMETHING
OTHER THAN OUR SELF

PICK YOURSELF UP – AND GET KNOCKED DOWN AGAIN

A few years after starting my new job, I was cruising through life again. It was as though the redundancy had never happened; it was simply a blip that no longer mattered. I was living with four friends in a big house in London where we sat around at weekends with hangovers, watching episodes of *Friends*. We were Friends. Life was good.

Then came the day I got my second big knock. My darling mother suddenly died. A brain aneurysm. She was just fifty-five and I went into shock. It turned out that the redundancy wasn't actually that bad. I could fix that. Now I was faced with something I couldn't fix.

My mother's death has affected my life every day since then. I am not who I was before. Big events such as the death of a parent can hit hard; they rock the foundations of our lives and make us question our own mortality, something I'd rarely thought about before.

I have friends who are very religious. They are more comfortable around death than I am, with firm beliefs about the afterlife and seeing loved ones again. I wish that I had religion in my life. But no matter how much I want to believe in God, I simply can't get there. I am spiritual and believe that there is something much greater than us, but the religion thing just isn't working for me.

SEARCHING FOR ANSWERS

I have spent years looking for ways to heal myself from the loss of my mother. I am always searching for answers, as well as studying how other cultures mourn their family. One of my ongoing struggles is why some people appear to be able to carry on as normal, relatively soon after losing someone, and why I feel this great sadness and grief years later. The British grieve in private, behind closed doors – there is no wailing in the church at the funeral or talk about the dead in the months that follow. We hold it together and crack on.

Which brings me onto the subject of animals. I promised you we would get there – thanks for bearing with me.

As well as learning about other cultures, I have also researched animals – the way that they deal with grief, the kindness they show their owners (and also each other) and how they can teach us to be more resilient.

When reading about resilience in animals, elephants always come up. Elephants live in close-knit herds, with a similar lifespan to humans. They form strong bonds and when one dies they mourn together. Mums have been known to mourn a stillborn calf and even to shed tears. But they are tough, and once they have mourned, they carry on together as a herd, supporting one another.

Elephants may be one of the only animals known to grieve, but I have read endless stories about cats and dogs showing clear signs of grief after their owners die. One story in particular stands out.

OSCAR, THE INTUITIVE CAT

In 2007, to many people's astonishment, the *New England Journal of Medicine* published a story about Oscar the cat, who was said to sense the imminent death of patients in a nursing home. Adopted as a kitten by the staff, Oscar roamed one floor of the Steere House nursing home, Rhode Island, USA, and over the course of several years, he curled up next to 50 patients, every one of whom had died shortly thereafter.

The staff were so sure of his ability that they would call up patients' relatives to encourage them to make a final visit. Doctors questioned whether Oscar could smell the chemicals released by dying cells, and while this couldn't be proven, both families and staff were grateful to Oscar for sitting with, and comforting patients during their final hours.

Oscar has even proved staff at the nursing home wrong. When nurses have thought they sensed the end for one of their patients and tried to take Oscar to them, he would refuse to sit, heading instead to other doors, where he would scratch and scratch until he was let in. Normally he has been right.

Oscar's story was documented and researched by Dr David Dosa, a geriatrician and university professor. Since publishing his article in 2007, Dr Dosa has

" "

THE KINDNESS
HE SHOWS CAN
MAKE END OF LIFE
FOR MANY A BETTER
EXPERIENCE THAN IT
WOULD HAVE BEEN
WITHOUT HIM

witnessed dozens more cases of Oscar sensing death in the nursing home and has written a book about him: *Making Rounds with Oscar: The Extraordinary Gift of an Ordinary Cat.*

Dr Dosa says that the main benefit to patients is the compassionate care Oscar gives to those who might otherwise die alone. The kindness he shows can make end of life for many a better experience than it would have been without him. With humans often resisting death itself, as well as any talk about it or being around people who are dying, it is interesting to see animals drawn to it, wanting to comfort and be close during the final hours.

CHLOE, THE CAT WITH NO TAIL

While I was grieving for my mum and searching for answers to the bigger questions in life, my father too had taken Mum's death badly and was struggling with depression. It is no great surprise to be depressed after a spouse's death, especially when you have been married to them for 30 years, but Mum was his second wife, and her death brought back the grief for his first wife as well. Dad's first wife died in her sleep from pneumonia in her 30s, leaving him with my older brother and sister. He used to say that losing one wife was unlucky, but two was careless.

Dad spent most of his time at home after Mum died. He would potter around the garden, tinkering with his beloved bonsai collection. He sat in his armchair watching sport and animal documentaries, looking out across our beautiful garden to the fields in the farmland beyond. Chloe the cat was his main companion.

When we got Chloe as a kitten, she was springy and cute. She loved being stroked and, along with her brother, Jabba, would play in the big garden, climbing trees and catching mice. Sadly, Jabba was killed by a car and Chloe would search for him for long periods afterward.

Chloe was so chubby that one day she got stuck when she tried to fit through the cat flap. It slammed shut on her tail, and she raced around the kitchen, blood spurting everywhere. We managed to catch her, wrap her in a towel and

75

rush her to the vet's. Unfortunately, she had to have her tail amputated, and I always think that it was this, perhaps along with the loss of her brother, that changed her nature as she got older.

Vastly overweight, Chloe did not appreciate being picked up or fussed over by anyone, but would not eat her food until Dad bent down to stroke her. Then, after some food and a stroke, her temperament changed from a cat who kept her distance to one who purred loudly, and she would weave her way between Dad's ankles. Perhaps the fact that she was at her best when being fed was the cause of her obesity. But Dad loved looking after her; it gave him a purpose.

"THE MORE KINDNESS WE GIVE OUT, THE MORE KINDNESS IS GENERATED "

It's no secret that we were not too fond of Chloe in old age. She was incontinent, she sprayed on the carpet and it began to make the house smell. Dad was not bothered by these things, claiming that he couldn't smell a thing. He was protective of her and wouldn't hear a bad word about her.

KINDNESS – THE ENERGETIC CURRENCY

After Mum's death, the roles shifted. My siblings and I would encourage Dad to get out more, to do some exercise and to eat less sugar. He was often cross with us about this, reminding us that he had managed fine on planet Earth for 70-odd years without us telling him what to do all the time. We could see him getting older and more unfit though, and simply wanted to slow the process down. Selfishly, we just wanted him to stick around for longer, and making those changes might have helped.

While he would often get cross with us, he never was with Chloe. They had a mutual respect for one another. He gave her food and stroked her and she reciprocated by purring and winding herself around his ankles or sitting on his armchair to keep it warm for him. They were kind to one another.

I talked to Kate Taylor, a creativity and empowerment coach:

.....

Kindness is an energetic currency that can never be spent. The more kindness we give out, the more kindness is generated. For example, if you let someone out in the traffic, you will notice that they will then stop to let someone in front of them out. When we do something with kindness, it has a positive benefit and we feel good. Doing something with kindness and compassion releases the happy hormone, oxytocin, into the brain and body, which, in turn, protects the heart by lowering blood pressure. Studies have shown that pets also produce oxytocin in the body; so, being kind to pets is a win–win for helping us to feel good and improve our health.

.....

Kate, owner of Bertie the dog, also discusses the emotional and physical benefits related to kindness:

.....

Animals teach us incredibly important empathy skills. Caring for a pet draws us away from the problems we may have in our own existence. Animals are constantly communicating through non-verbal cues, such as body language and facial expressions. Therefore, we are able to think about what their needs are, and what we can do to help them. They take us out of our own self to put a focus on the needs of something other than our self.

.....

IT'S OK TO NOT BE OK

Kindness can promote gratitude. Dad was always the first person to go and visit a friend. The minute he found out they were in hospital, he sprang into action. He had to think of someone else; it took him out of his depression. With Chloe, he had the same response. He would get up from his chair to let her in and out of the house, to feed her, to stroke her. He had that responsibility and she was a companion to him. For this we were grateful. Chloe also allowed him to be grumpy, without being told to cheer up. He could moan, with only purring for a response. It was OK for him not to be OK. Dad and Chloe both taught me this – and it's an important part of learning how to grieve.

Pets can teach us about resilience and how to get through tough events in life. They are accepting and allow us to be as we are. There is no judgment – only unconditional love.

TIME TO SLOW DOWN

Ali Carrington is a reiki practitioner. Having been very sporty, she found it difficult to accept when she was diagnosed with ME. Resting or slowing down was not in her character and she was fighting it with everything she had. The problem was that with ME you need to rest. In fact, it is crucial. Simple things that she could have done previously took a whole new level of energy and Ali struggled to deal with this, mentally as well as physically.

Enter Kenny, the ten-year-old rescue boxer. Ali took Kenny into her home just after she was diagnosed with ME. She does not know the full extent of what happened to Kenny in his first ten years of life, but it's safe to say that it wasn't great. He was scared of going outside, disliked being left alone for more than an hour at a time, if at all. He was fearful of many things, but also had a stoic demeanour.

Kenny taught Ali to slow down. She had to stay at home more because he was scared of going outside. Invitations were turned down because dogs were not welcome and Kenny hated being left alone. Ali was learning to say no to things; it made her re-evaluate what was important and even led to her purchasing a house in the countryside to visit as often as possible with Kenny. They chose the house because they thought that Kenny would like it: no nearby busy roads, and peace and quiet all around.

Ali runs a dog-listening company, helping families improve their relationships with their dogs. She has dealt with all sorts of issues, from aggression toward humans or other dogs, to chewing up the house when left alone, separation

" "

CHLOE ALSO
ALLOWED HIM
TO BE GRUMPY,
WITHOUT BEING
TOLD TO CHEER
UP. HE COULD
MOAN, WITH ONLY
PURRING FOR
A RESPONSE

anxiety or pulling on the lead. Kenny was her biggest challenge yet. During their three and a half years together before Kenny died, they experienced moments of understanding and calm and it was truly joyful. These moments gradually became more frequent until, finally, they became his new normal. Because of her experience with Kenny, Ali now works closely with a boxer-welfare charity on some of their most challenging cases, as well as with other dog-welfare associations.

SIT AND BE STILL

I am still learning daily how to work my way through grief. I do know that all around us there are people and animals to help us, to teach us things and to show us that everything will be OK. Cats and dogs can help all of us through difficult periods in life. And you don't need to own one to experience the benefits, as I found out from the stories of Oscar.

Animals appear to be very intuitive. They can sense if we have low vitality or mood and give out the energy that we may need. On a walk, I will stop to sit and listen to the birds, being still until they get closer, realizing that I am there and showing me their inquisitive sides.

The school run is along a beach boardwalk. There are dogs everywhere. I often sit on the bench and watch them racing along the sand, running back to their owners with a ball and witnessing the love between the two, totally present in that moment.

They teach us about resilience. When we see how animals bounce back from illness, loss and neglect, their actions remind and encourage us to do the same.

PAWS FOR THOUGHT

Managing life's plot twists

1 | GO ANIMAL WATCHING
Make time to watch animals around you. Observe their behaviours and see what you can learn from them.

2 | BE KIND…
…to those around you, animals, dogs that come racing up to you in the park panting with joy. Pick up on their excitement and grab some for yourself. The more you give out, the more you receive.

3 | IT'S OK NOT TO BE OK
We often try to fight something, when the best thing is to accept it and wait for this time to pass.

4 | SLOW DOWN
We all need some slow times. This could be as simple as going outside and observing birds in the sky. Remind yourself that all is well in the world.

5 | LEARN FROM THEM
There are so many heart-warming stories about incredible acts of kindness and resilience shown by animals. Go to the library or search online to find some stories and learn more.

6 | KEEP GOING
Remember that everything will be OK – because it will, eventually. Animals keep going, we keep going. Think of challenges as simply plot twists in the story of life.

THE DOLITTLE

EFFECT

CHAPTER 6

THE DOLITTLE EFFECT

From talking to gracious listening

Philosopher, Dr Brennan Jacoby | Founder of Philosophy at Work

As a child, I couldn't help but be drawn in by the pure, unbridled curiosity conveyed by the stories of Dr Dolittle. As a city boy transplanted to the country at the age of eight, living on a small farm with more animals than friends, for me the prospect of talking to animals was thrilling.

To be more specific, when we moved, we brought my hamster, Isiah Thomas (named after my basketball hero) and my dog, Coconut – a golden Labrador – with us, and then added about 13 chickens, three goats, four ducks, six pigs and two cats. It's fair to say it wasn't exactly a commercial farm.

For what I'm going to share with you, it's also important to say that when I was eight and living on our farm, I was home-schooled. My parents were both professional musicians, but they also had teaching degrees, and so the arrangement was legal. But because none of us had ever done anything like this before, the experience was, at the start, shall we say, fairly organic. Structured lessons were interspersed with goat-milking. And it was normal to be faced with mathematical story problems about how many omelets we could make per calendar month if each chicken laid an average of five eggs a week and every omelet required two. I'm still figuring that one out. But most of all, the blending of education and animals impressed on me the possibility of not just talking to animals but learning from them.

Growing up with animals made me ask a lot of questions: why does a billy goat headbutt his mates? Do pigs appreciate being fed as much as they seem to? And where is my hamster?

" "

BY LISTENING
GRACIOUSLY, IT IS
AS IF THE LISTENING
DOG IS SAYING,
"I KNOW YOU
STUTTER WHEN YOU
READ, BUT I DON'T
MIND. IN FACT, IT'S
MUSIC TO MY EARS"

As a philosopher, I still ask a lot of questions, but recently, a particular group of dogs has reawakened my animal-based tutelage. The lessons I am learning from them feel more than therapeutic.

Now that I am a young husband and father managing my own business in the frenetic culture of London, England, these lessons feel more like much-needed flotation devices that help keep my nose above water. And I don't think I'm alone. You don't have to be married, a parent or work in a city to need a life preserver thrown to you every now and again. I'm not sure if the world has changed or I've just grown up, but things are now moving very fast. The fear of the unknown no longer feels theoretical. For many of us, things do just feel less secure.

So, grab your favourite dog (or cat or snake), move the fish tank a bit closer and get comfortable. Because the things I'm learning from dogs are not just therapeutic. I think they go directly to the heart of the ailments with which many of us are living today.

First things first: I have to tell you about the dogs.

MEET DANNY

Danny is a professional dog. He and his owner, Tony Nevett, live in England and work all around the country. A blue-and-white greyhound, Danny's job is to go with Tony into schools and listen to children read as part of the Bark and Read programme with the Kennel Club (the UK's largest organization dedicated to the welfare of dogs). Danny and Tony were the first to do this kind of work in Europe, but the reading-assistance dog movement they belong to has been going on for some time in the USA.

The use of listening dogs is part of a well-established group of pet-based therapies. In the late 1700s, psychiatrists at The Retreat in the north of England gave patients responsibility for the care of rabbits and poultry as part of their therapy. About 30 years later, Florence Nightingale advised that small pets could make good companions for the chronically ill. She herself even kept a pet owl, named Athena, in her apron pocket until she went off to the Crimean

War. And in the 1960s, the child psychologist Boris Levinson described the presence of dogs as a "social lubricant", helping children to come out of their shells and connect with each other.

With research estimating that over 70 percent of children of all ages talk to, and confide in, animals, teams like Danny and Tony are certainly well placed and relevant. But the positive difference they make, and the lessons they are teaching me, are not just about the benefits of having animals around. Something special happens when people start talking to these dogs.

THE DOLITTLE EFFECT IN ACTION

Scientific studies have proven what many of us know intuitively, and what I will call the Dolittle Effect: talking to dogs is good for you.

One group of researchers at Indiana University of Pennsylvania found that literacy levels increased more significantly when children read to dogs than when they read to their peers. The dogs' presence seemed to give the students both the courage and the confidence to do something that usually made them feel vulnerable.

The change that dogs bring about in the children who read to them is what first caught my attention, and made me wonder what they might have to teach us about how to listen to each other ourselves. And by following that line of thinking, I discovered two lessons. These lessons can not only help us to be better listeners – they can also prove therapeutic when life gets difficult.

Lesson One: passive is powerful

When I first spoke with Tony Nevett about the work he and Danny do in schools, I asked him what enabled the dog to have such a positive impact on children. I expected him to say that it all boiled down to Danny's training, temperament or breed. Or perhaps it was really about Tony, and his ability to support students. But instead, and I'll admit somewhat disappointingly, Tony said that there was nothing particularly special about Danny. When I asked if any one breed made better listening dogs, Tony simply said he worked with greyhounds because their short hair was better in terms of allergies. In fact,

" "

IT CAN SEEM
THAT FOR
SOMETHING
TO BE TRULY
THERAPEUTIC
IT MUST BE AS
COMPLICATED
AS THE
CHALLENGE
IT IS USED
TO HELP

he went so far as to say that there was nothing special about dogs, and that there could, he thought, probably be listening rabbits or listening cats as well.

I suspect that the fact that Tony's answer was disappointing to me says more about my expectations of therapy than anything else. And again, I think I'm probably not alone. It can seem that for something to be truly therapeutic it must be as complicated as the challenge it is used to help. Maybe it is that the scary or difficult thing in our own minds feels so difficult or so large that we want to make sure we bring something equally robust to the fight. And so, Tony's answer let me down because I assumed listening dogs had nothing useful to teach me if they used no complex strategy or theory. But in fact, the truth is that what makes listening dogs so therapeutic is that they listen in a way that is simply and beautifully passive, rather than active.

Passivity tends to be looked down upon today. It seems better to be active and assertive. How else would anything ever get done? How else could we help our friends and family when they are in need? How else can we help ourselves? In fact, if I'm honest, if I were in the position of a listening dog, I would actively strive to be a "good" listener. And before meeting the listening dogs, I would have thought that meant I should practise "active listening".

Active listening is the act of listening out for the emotional message someone is implicitly or explicitly communicating to you before repeating back to them what you have heard. It is known to be a very therapeutic way to listen. By showing someone that you have not just heard the words they have spoken, but also the feelings they communicated, you help them to feel heard and known. I have found active listening to be a very positive practice in my own life, and so I was surprised to find that listening dogs provide a therapeutic presence by listening passively – in precisely the opposite way.

Dogs like Danny are unable to practise active listening, to give answers or coach the children who are reading to them. And that is their strength. They help by simply being a dog; by just showing up as they are. I find that deeply cheering. It means that when my family, friends and colleagues confide in me and need support, I don't have to have all the answers or to try and fix them. I can listen well and care for them just by being present.

The benefits of passive listening extend to self-care as well.

When I am angry, sad, anxious or confused, my usual response is to interrogate my feelings in the hope of understanding them, sorting them out and moving on to a more pleasurable state. But that is not what listening dogs do.

If I were to be a bit more like Danny with myself, I would try to make space to first just allow the difficult emotions to exist. I am not a psychologist or therapist. I am a philosopher. But in my experience, I can say that recognizing the emotions that are present within me, and accepting that they are there – at least in that moment – is an important part of taking care of myself.

The passive listening displayed by listening dogs is a good reminder of just how powerful and positive it can be to sit with whatever is going on.

"I CAN LISTEN WELL AND CARE FOR THEM JUST BY BEING PRESENT"

In this life, with its busyness, responsibilities and expectations, it is nice to strike on something that is therapeutic without adding to my to-do list. In fact, listening to others and to myself like a listening dog takes items off that list. I need only be present.

The curious thing, though, about listening dogs is that despite all this, they do not appear to be purely passive. It does seem that they have some choice in the matter, that they don't have to listen – and this is significant for the next lesson I am learning from them.

Lesson Two: give up the gavel
The passive listening that dogs like Danny display is powerful because it can be received as a form of acceptance. It is non-judgmental because, of course, a dog can't judge like a human does. Freud famously thought his dog, a chow named Jofi, was skilled at assessing the state of his analysands. But regardless of what dogs may pick up about humans, it seems safe to assume they are not

capable of judging us in the critical way in which we can judge each other. That is, they can't dish out shame. Danny isn't going to roll his eyes and tut because little Johnny is struggling to read a sentence; he's not going to joke with other dogs behind Johnny's back.

And yet, the listening that these dogs do *feels* non-judgmental. It feels like they are looking past our flaws and accepting, even loving us in our vulnerability. The listening they offer may not be active, but it does feel gracious. And that is incredibly and powerfully therapeutic. This is what I think makes it more helpful to talk to a dog than to talk to a picture of one or to a robot dog. Animals like dogs seem to have enough choice and personality that when they sit with us it feels like they want to be there.

"THEY ARE NOT CAPABLE OF JUDGING US IN THE CRITICAL WAY IN WHICH WE CAN JUDGE EACH OTHER"

By listening graciously, it is as if the listening dog is saying, "I know you stutter when you read, but I don't mind. In fact, it's music to my ears."

So here is what I think makes these listening dogs so important: without even trying, they communicate to us that the very thing we think means we are a failure is not the end of the world. With this, listening dogs bring perspective. They remind us that the part of us we might think we should hide is nothing to be ashamed of. They are happy to sit with us just as we are.

Take a moment to let that sink in.

When was the last time you sat with someone who made you feel your perceived flaws were acceptable and even lovable? This is the way that listening dogs help make life beautiful. They do not only listen in a powerfully passive and seemingly gracious way; their very existence stands to remind us to listen to ourselves – and each other – in equally gracious ways.

BUT WHAT IF YOU'RE NOT A DOG?

If you're like me, you might be thinking that these lessons are all well and good – you might even feel motivated to try bringing more passivity and grace into your listening – but there may be a niggling critique in the back of your mind saying: "But I'm not a dog! It's easy for Danny to listen without judging if he simply can't judge. But I can; and, in fact, I think the human ability to reason and assess is a real strength." And I would agree with you.

The ancient Greek philosopher Aristotle famously argued that the thing that sets humans apart from other animals is that we are rational. We have the capacity to think about thinking, and that is a good thing.

Rather than the pursuit of passive, gracious listening, meaning that we must switch off one of our more honourable faculties, I want to suggest that our gift of reason makes the impact of any passive and gracious listening all the more beautiful. If you and I manage not to blink or run for the hills when a friend divulges their darkest secrets to us, we are offering a gracious gift. The same goes for when we sit patiently with our own difficulties, embarrassments and challenges.

When we manage to truly accept ourselves and others, we are giving something with powerful therapeutic potential – because, unlike dogs, *we have a capacity for doing otherwise*. When we choose grace over shame, we offer love to others; we offer love to ourselves.

A LOVELY WORLD?

What we learn from the listening dogs is that sometimes therapy is fairly unassuming. We can help ourselves and others by simply showing up, receiving what is being said, and choosing to respond with grace. It is about feeling safe enough to embrace our own imperfections and limitations.

This does not mean we are powerless to change and grow, or that we should not strive to stretch ourselves and shake off unhelpful habits or addictions. It is just a reminder that we should balance all that striving with a good dose of simply being here as we are.

In the well-known song from the 1967 movie, Dr Dolittle supposes that if he could just talk to the animals, the world would be a lovely place. I wouldn't want to contradict the good doctor, but the lessons listening dogs offer suggest a different world, in fact. If we listen passively and with grace, the world itself may not become much lovelier. There will still be pain, anger and confusion. But we will be much better equipped to live in it and talk, and listen, to each other. After all, we are animals, too.

PAWS FOR THOUGHT

Listening like a dog

1 | EARS
You already have everything
you need to listen well.
Simply being present can
make a positive difference.

2 | PAUSE
Make time for things to sink
in before responding. With
the best of intentions, it can
be tempting to rush in with
advice. Whether listening
to others or yourself, taking
a moment is time well spent.

3 | YOU
The very thing you think
means you are a failure might
be precisely what helps you
add value to the world.

4 | QUESTION
When in doubt, wait or ask
a question. Honest questions
driven by authentic curiosity
can help show that you are
listening with care.

CHAPTER 7

BELONGING

BELONGING

Connecting with others through animals

Clare Barry | Founder of Urban Curiosity

In 2017, Dr Helen Stokes-Lampard – Chair of the UK's Royal College of General Practitioners – said that loneliness can be as bad for our health as diseases such as diabetes or high blood pressure. Meanwhile, research conducted by the London School of Economics and the Campaign to End Loneliness (a London-based group of charities) found that the impact on our health of social isolation is equivalent to smoking 15 cigarettes a day. We are more connected than ever – we've got mobile phones, the Internet, social media – yet we're experiencing an epidemic of loneliness. Many of us live away from our families; we often work alone from home or the local coffee shop; some of us prioritize our education, careers and financial stability over being in relationships. It's more common for us to be urbanites; life in our towns and cities is fast.

As we spend more time engaging with each other online, opportunities for human connection can be harder to find. Real-world contact with people and a sense of belonging are critical to our mental and physical wellbeing. How can pets help root us in our communities, and can they help us gain a sense of belonging?

GET OUT OF THE HOUSE

In 2015, I moved back into the family home to care for my mother who had stage-four blood cancer. That summer my world shrank, as I learned to fit in with Mum's timetable of medications and naps, only leaving the house for her hospital appointments. The sole bit of normality in each day – when I was just me, rather than the daughter/carer/advocate version – was saying hello to our

" "

IN A WORLD
WHERE WE FOLLOW
AND CONNECT
WITH STRANGERS
VIRTUALLY, ANIMALS
OPEN UP SPACE FOR
CONVERSATIONS
IN REAL LIFE

next-door neighbours over the front-garden fence. I noticed they seemed to know everyone who passed by and I found it perplexing. How did they have such a connection with so many locals when they'd only moved in a few years before, whereas my family had lived on the street for decades and barely seemed to know anyone?

My friends next door were crazy about each other and animals in equal measure. Their jobs involved frequent international travel, which prevented them from having their own pets, but they adored greeting every canine who sauntered by their gate. They encouraged local cats to visit too, for treats and cuddles, and made friends with their owners. When they were home, Honky Tonk, a sophisticated Siamese, was a regular visitor and recipient of their attention and kitty goodies. And, I watched how, by extension, a friendship developed between them and the feckless feline's owners. Lingering on the doorstep within earshot of my mother gave me small moments of happiness at a time when a walk in the park was not possible for me. A smile, a sunset, the roses blooming, a lazy miaow, a warm breeze – all simple pleasures and a helpful reminder of life and beauty outside the lonesome bubble I inhabited.

A SENSE OF BELONGING

In a world where we follow and connect with strangers virtually, animals open up space for conversations in real life. It doesn't have to be about anything profound, but it can help us feel more human and less alone. A sense of belonging can ease the challenges of loneliness. "It's a human need, just like the need for food and shelter. Feeling that you belong is most important in seeing value in life and in coping with intensely painful emotions," reported Dr Karyn Hall, psychologist and author, writing in the American magazine *Psychology Today*. When pet owners meet, they already have something in common. The dog at the end of a leash makes it so much easier for someone to form a bond with a stranger. If you are new to an area, you will find out about great vets and GPs, where to pick up a delicious coffee and who's the best yoga teacher far quicker by walking your dog in the park than you would via a digital noticeboard. A passion for pups seems to be an invitation to join a community with ease.

After Mum died, I tried to get my life back on track and went for afternoon walks with my friends from next door in our local park. A 30-minute stroll took an hour because they stopped to pet every animal we passed, exchanging brief pleasantries with the owners before moving on. There was Rudy, the Cockador puppy with a golden coat covered in stinky fox excrement. (She loved to roll in it, her owner explained with a despairing eye roll.) A Great Dane called Edgar enjoyed playing with her owner's grandchildren and they squealed with delight as she messed around with them on the grass. Meanwhile, I loved watching a tiny sausage dog named Margo chase squirrels like she was possessed, and Ritzo, the five-month-old Jack Russell, skitter along the pavement. The weeks melted into months and I began to feel part of something. I shared a small piece of my identity with these people who called this area their home, like me.

> ## "IT'S A HUMAN NEED, JUST LIKE THE NEED FOR FOOD AND SHELTER. FEELING THAT YOU BELONG IS MOST IMPORTANT IN SEEING VALUE IN LIFE AND IN COPING WITH INTENSELY PAINFUL EMOTIONS"

The funny thing is, I never knew any of their names. They were just a series of somebodies with a pooch. Yet there was something refreshing about this openness and friendliness that was free from the unspoken rules of other social settings. It made me less self-conscious and happier to chat about inconsequential topics. It gave me moments of feeling normal at a time when life seemed anything but, and I felt like I was going mad with grief. In the park, during those conversations, no one was watching my expression or listening for the catch in my voice or assessing the subtext of my words. I was simply one of a trio of adults petting the furry creatures gallivanting in the park. And playing with the dogs got me out of my head and into the present moment. I felt light and happy as I tossed a ball across the field and watched one of my new four-legged friends bound after it.

" "

OUR PERSONAL
RESILIENCE IS
INTERWOVEN INTO
RESILIENCE OF THE
COMMUNITIES TO
WHICH WE BELONG

HUMAN CONNECTION

I grew up in a house with my mother and brother and no cats or dogs. Over the years, we had an assortment of goldfish and, for a while, we had a black-and-tan mini rabbit, thoughtfully named Thumper. This might explain why I had no idea there were gatherings and dog-walking weekends run by meet-up groups like Explore by Paw or social dog clubs until recently. For anyone who's introverted or socially anxious, perhaps depressed or shy, a canine can be the ultimate icebreaker. The crucial thing is, this four-legged animal can connect us with others in a relaxed way and this is good for our mental health. Our need to belong is about feeling accepted, receiving attention or support and giving this to others in return. You could argue that these exchanges in my community were all rather superficial. To an extent, this is true. Pet owners rarely talk about themselves – they're simply a man or woman with a beloved animal – and yet they are witnessed by another human being, even if the interaction is a simple nod of the head in passing. "In order to feel connected, we need to feel seen, heard and valued," said Baya Voce, relationship expert and NLP practitioner, speaking about connection in a TED Talk at TEDxSaltLakeCity in the US. In "The Simple Cure for Loneliness", which has been viewed nearly 3 million times, Baya makes the case for ritual as a key to connection. She is not talking about the spiritual or sacred, but:

.....

...instead, something that we're already doing on a day-to-day basis. The key to making ritual such a powerful tool for connection is that ritual is repeated action plus intention. When you combine [these], ritual becomes ingrained in you just like habits do. The best places to find ritual are with your friends and families, and your intimate relationships and within your communities.

.....

What's interesting is how the habits and rhythms of having to walk the dog, for example, mean the same people encounter each other one or more times a day, and this can foster a sense of belonging and reassuring familiarity. My aunt has a terrier called Hughie. The people she knows from the doggie community in her area know nothing of her past profession or her preoccupations, and yet they see her more often than she sees her dearest friends. This contact is positive and also allows her to be freer with her identity. There's no status or expectation involved in her exchanges with other dog owners, no preconceptions about who or what she is – in that moment, she is simply Hughie's owner. Even clothing and footwear tend to be chosen for their practical qualities, not for fashion-statement potential. Animals can help us enjoy all the benefits of human connection and the feeling of being part of something without any burden to perform or be viewed in a certain way. It is an important antidote to disconnection and loneliness.

Our ageing population has grown by nearly half in the past 30 years and while people are enjoying retirement for longer, many are suffering with loneliness. And it's not just the older generation who crave human connection: freelancers, stay-at-home mothers, carers, the unemployed, newcomers to an area and asylum seekers can all experience the damaging impact of isolation. "Our personal resilience is interwoven into resilience of the communities to which we belong. It is from the web of our relationships and connections with other people that we draw our strength. Such communities can lift us when we are down and give us the capacity to deal with whatever challenges come our way," said Dr John Sharry, a social worker and psychologist writing in the *Irish Times*.

Animals can connect us to other humans. When we take dogs for a walk we encounter other people in real life, which allows us to interpret all the non-verbal signals they give off. It is all these tiny clues that help us build relationships and develop the bonds we need to feel a sense of belonging – these are things that we can't detect when we interact with other humans online. It is all these tiny clues that help us build relationships and develop the bonds we need to feel a sense of belonging. Feeling we are part of something greater than ourselves is key to belongingness, and pets can help us with this. Angus, for example, is my friend and fellow freelancer's Airedale terrier, and he does more than just force Daniel to leave the house. Angus's boundless enthusiasm will inevitably draw comment from a passer-by, and so his owner engages in a conversation, which may be inconsequential or, indeed, the start of something bigger and more meaningful.

EMBRACE DIVERSITY

While a love of dogs may bring other dog lovers onto our radars, what is not a given is that they'll share our politics or cultural heritage or religion. I like that my London street has people from all over the world living on it – from Australia, Switzerland, Barbados, Italy, Singapore, France, Brazil, India, Poland, Spain, Somalia, Philippines, Canada, Ireland, Greece and all over the UK. I know this through the conversations I've had in the neighbourhood. Those walks with my next-door neighbour exposed me to dogs and their owners, the latter who were different from me in every way except for where we lived. Yet these days, we connect more than ever with "people like us", rather than those who actually share our streets. The Internet is filtering what we see by what it wants us to see. We consume content that confirms the views we already hold and connects us with people who look and think like us. "It's a problem", says Eli Pariser, author of *The Filter Bubble: What the Internet is Hiding from You*, "because it means you're less likely than ever to be confronted with information that challenges your views, or gets you out of your comfort zone. Your own point of view follows you wherever you go."

It's so important to know and relate to our diverse communities – to get back in touch with what others actually think, even if we don't agree. It can help promote empathy and understanding. It might even prompt us to reassess our own lives and make us feel grateful for our lot, and this is important for our mental health. Research published in the journal *Personality and Individual Differences* showed that people were more aware of self-care and wellbeing-boosting behaviours – good nutrition, sleep, regular movement – when they were grateful for experiences, relationships or things. Pets offer us the opportunity to be present and, potentially, to embrace and celebrate the life we have. This sense of peace and contentment is crucial to positive mental health.

DISCOVER YOUR COMMUNITY

Just before Christmas 2017, my friend from next door died unexpectedly. She was 57 years old. Her husband is bereft and now it's me persuading him to come to the park. He wonders about what the future holds; he doesn't know if he can bear to return to work. (They worked on a married roster for the same airline for years and were rarely apart, whether in the air or on the ground.)

Out walking together, we follow the path by the allotments and the football field. He pets every pooch we see – as he has always done. I tentatively mention Borrow My Doggy. He looks contemplative for the first time in weeks.

Established in 2012, the company connects dog owners with trusted local dog lovers to share the care of their dogs. Rikke Rosenlund, the company's founder, knew many dog owners planning a holiday or working long hours who could not afford kennels or dog-sitters, or who resisted using such services because they felt their beloved animals did not get enough attention in these settings. This inspired her to create a way for people without dogs, like her, to enjoy all the benefits of one.

> ## "IT'S SO IMPORTANT TO KNOW AND RELATE TO OUR DIVERSE COMMUNITIES – TO GET BACK IN TOUCH WITH WHAT OTHERS ACTUALLY THINK, EVEN IF WE DON'T AGREE"

From the elderly man recovering from surgery who needed help with exercising his pet to the depressed woman who found the match helpful in enabling her to get out and have some social contact in the process of getting healthy again, the company is all about wellbeing and friendship with animals and humans. It might be the perfect thing for my bereaved friend in this time of uncertainty and sorrow.

Rikke tells me about a woman who was worried her daughter was struggling to adapt to life at university; then the student borrowed a dog and established positive routines for her mental and physical health.

Parents of younger children concerned about their screen time have reconnected with their kids thanks to a borrowed dog. "Where the children were once closed off and focused on their devices after school, now they go for walks with their parents and share the events of their day," explains Rikke.

I am inspired to learn how Borrow My Doggy has helped people to connect with other locals. Rikke tells me about a dog owner who had just had a baby and was matched with a family across the street who had a five-year-old son. "The son begged for a dog, but his father is allergic to them. The mother grew up with dogs and she really wanted some dog time in her and her son's life, so borrowing their neighbour's pooch was the perfect solution. The two women developed a firm friendship that survived the dog owner having a second baby and moving away."

Rikke and her team have created a way for people to connect with themselves and each other without a single penny being exchanged. The platform allows busy people to relax without the ongoing responsibility of looking after a pet. "Getting some headspace and spending some time together is so good for your mental state, especially if you have a high-pressured job. It's quite nice to switch off and have that time to yourself," explained one member. "Borrow My Doggy has made me feel more connected to the community. It's a win-win," said another.

But perhaps the most striking endorsement of the power of Borrow My Doggy is a comment from Toby, the owner of Scout, a lively springer spaniel: "It creates such a wonderful basis for a community because you're all sharing something that exudes love. A great dog is just the embodiment of a good love." This is just what my friend needs right now because animals are the antidote to loneliness. They keep us company, but also bring us into contact with other people and give us a shared experience. This is positive for our mental health and, of course, the physical activity involved with walking a dog is beneficial too.

Companies like Borrow My Doggy mean all of us can enjoy animals, even if our lifestyle prohibits us from owning one. We need to draw on the power of community and feel like we belong. Animals make this possible.

PAWS FOR THOUGHT

Ideas for connecting through animals

1 | AN INVITATION

Animals offer us an invitation to become part of a community. We build bonds and gain friends through the shared love of a four-legged creature. Whether you own a pet or not, making the most of the invitation to connect provided by a furry friend can help link you to your community in simple ways.

2 | BELONGING

As humans, we need to feel we belong to something, and pets can make this possible wherever we are. Making time to find something positive that we belong to beyond work is time well spent.

3 | RITUAL CONNECTION

The regular dog walk at a set time of the day allows owners to acknowledge one another. How many familiar faces do you pass regularly each day? Perhaps without even owning a pet you could offer a nod, smile or "morning" to one of those people. It might begin a connection akin to the dog owner's bond.

4 | BORROW MY DOG

For those of us without a furry friend what might happen with a reach out to someone else's pet? From dog fostering to the occasional dog walk to help out a neighbour you may find unexpected friendships that cross many social barriers.

CHAPTER 8

PETS AT WORK

PETS AT WORK

The best therapist has fur and four legs

Kate Peers | Author of the blog *Mad about the boys*

Can you imagine attending a school with goats on the campus? And not only on campus, but playing a big part in the school day? Goats that have been known to break into the food supplies, escape into classrooms, perhaps even cause the odd corridor evacuation. Yet they are loved, the source of envy of children at nearby schools and of bonding, bringing teenagers together at a time when they need it the most.

112

Teenagers can have many issues, including low self-esteem. While it can be normal for a teenager to lack confidence or be disappointed in themselves, people with self-esteem issues often view themselves as unable and unworthy.

Low self-esteem can be particularly hard for young people as they're exposed to new life events, like starting high school and forming new friendships and relationships. Teenagers face a host of pressures, from the changes of puberty to questions about who they are and where they fit in. With all this turmoil and uncertainty, it isn't always easy to differentiate between normal teenage behaviour and depression. Fortunately, once identified, it's treatable and schools can help. And one British school has discovered that having goats around creates more benefits than simply keeping the grass down.

VARNDEAN GOATS

Varndean School in Sussex, England, has six goats living on campus full-time. The school holds goat club every lunchtime with students and staff who all take great pleasure in learning about the goats, caring for them and cleaning their

" "

WHILE YOU THINK
YOU ARE CARING
FOR THEM, THEY
ARE ACTUALLY
CARING FOR YOU

home. The kids take so much from the club and one boy hasn't missed a single lunchtime feeding and grooming them. The goats are so popular they even have their own Twitter account (@varndeangoats), run by the goats themselves (a genius idea and very funny to follow).

Hilary Goldsmith, director of finance at Varndean, originally thought of getting goats to keep the grass down in a certain area of the school grounds. She is heavily involved in the goat club. "The goats are very naughty at times, they steal food and break into stuff. This can really help children with behavioural issues; they can see that they aren't the worst behaved in the school.

"STUDENTS CAN LEARN ABOUT MINDFULNESS THROUGH NURTURING AND CARING FOR THE ANIMALS"

"The goats are continually doing naughty things. My office is next door to the goat quad. We store their food in here after they broke into every food bin we tried. Now, when anyone tries to go out of the door they collectively try to barge their way into the corridor and stampede my office, looking for the food bin. Assembly has been delayed because we have had to hold back 300 students while we get the goats out of my office and back into the quad."

The goats have eaten homework, application forms, governors' minutes and even hoof-marked the rather smart coats of important visitors. They have pooped on the head teacher's carpet, been to assembly, been evacuated in a fire drill and are utterly devoid of all morals and remorse. Still, they are dearly loved by teachers and students alike and the goats love them all back.

At the heart of Varndean goats is animal therapy. The school believes that children often lose touch with animals as they grow up. Schools might have a hamster or similar pet for younger classes, but this is rare in high schools. Goat club offers older children and teenagers opportunities to learn about animal care and nurture at the same time.

The goat area is also a quiet place for children to visit during the day. Communication can be whatever is needed: verbal, non-verbal, a friendly headbutt or a furry hug. Children often go there for friendship, whether two- or four-legged; as they say at Varndean: friendship doesn't count feet.

Many rebellious and unhealthy behaviours or attitudes in teenagers can be indications of depression. Depression can destroy the essence of a teen's personality, causing an overwhelming sense of sadness, despair or anger. It can also cause low energy and concentration difficulties. At school, this may lead to poor attendance, a drop in grades or frustration with schoolwork.

The staff can see the benefits that animal therapy brings to their pupils. Behavioural incidents have gone down by 29 percent for the same period a year previously since the goats were introduced. But their real purpose is to calm children down in a quiet, outdoor space. Students can learn about mindfulness through nurturing and caring for the animals.

Goat club, which anyone can join, happens every lunchtime. Children learn responsibility, kindness and teamwork, along with animal care too. Varndean run a programme through which students can apply to be goat leaders, and many who they thought would be too shy to apply have put themselves through a proper interview process and the scrutiny of their peers. Through this, they have developed into confident and skilled young people, able to lead groups, plan trips, fundraise and represent their school locally and in the national media.

Children also talk about seeing their teachers in a different light when they all head out to goat club. They find that their temperaments are calmer and that they are often more gentle than when they are teaching and maintaining discipline in the classroom.

The school uses the goat quad as a space to de-escalate behaviour in children who may be reacting to something. Teenagers who may be struggling with depression or just finding their way at school use goat club when they need some escape. The animals act as therapists in their own way, calming children, distracting them and providing amusement during stressful times.

The goats tend to run off when a child comes outside angry; this inspires them to calm down, so they don't frighten the animals and, in turn, it encourages them to regulate their behaviour.

Students know that the goats will always be welcoming and friendly, so whatever circumstances they might find themselves in, they will always be sure of a friendly headbutt in the goat quad. They can also learn about forgiveness, and see that love is still there, even when naughty behaviour has happened.

THE DOOGLERS OF GOOGLE

A company that is frequently rated the best place to work in the USA is Google. They have slides in their offices, free healthy staff meals, free laundry and childcare. Google made the decision to be a "dog company" and to exclude cats in their work code of conduct. Their statement on the matter is as follows:

.....

Google's affection for our canine friends is an integral facet of our corporate culture. We like cats, but we're a dog company, so as a general rule we feel cats visiting our offices would be fairly stressed out.

.....

Google allows supervised dogs in the office, and frequent visitors even get their own badges. They say that it embodies the "tenacity, loyalty and all-round playfulness" of their company culture. "As long as they respect the no-peeing-on-the-carpets policy." Dog lovers can join the "Dooglers" – a group of canine-loving Google employees – and visit a dog-themed café on site.

Staff are more likely to stay at work longer, as they aren't worried about their pet being alone. Plus, it saves them paying for dog-walkers and also brings fun and energy into the workplace.

Google aren't the only company with dogs in the office.

THE ADVENTURES OF ROLO AND COOPER

I work for a company called Digital Mums. A few months after my third child was born, I began thinking about getting back to work and how that would be for us as a family. My previous life in an advertising agency wouldn't work for my new life with three children. I wanted to be there to pick them up from school and cuddle up with them at home if they were poorly. I struggled to find the solution, until one day I read about Digital Mums in an online forum.

The goal at Digital Mums is to support every mum to achieve their perfect work/life balance – something they call #Workthatworks. They train up mums with in-demand digital skills to help them create stimulating, flexible careers that fit around family life. I finished the course over two years ago and, since then, I have worked for a range of clients including a tourist board, a newspaper, a forest school and a variety of shops. All of my work is done from home and I'm now also employed by Digital Mums as a social-media guide, helping other mums on the same journey. Again, I am remote, but the team is a very close one and Rolo and Mr Coop, Co-Heads of Snuggles, are part of the reason we are all such a great team.

Digital Mums' founders, Kathryn Tyler and Nikki Cochrane, bring their dogs into the office and meetings as standard. Mr Coop, the English bull terrier and Rolo, the French bulldog puppy, play huge roles in the business and even have their own mugshots on the website's team page. It lends the company a sense of fun and community.

With many of the team working remotely, the dogs are part of the weekly online updates and will often be snoring in the background or filmed sleeping at the co-founders' feet. It makes staff laugh and brings us all together. Our quarterly meet-ups frequently end with us singing karaoke at the Digital Mums offices, with Rolo and Mr Coop nearby, relaxing.

Take a break

Occasionally, running your own business can be a lonely place. The buck stops with you and you are the only one who can resolve things. On a day with low energy, however, a dog at work will pick you up; while you think you are caring for them, they are actually caring for you.

Nikki describes the long working hours of an entrepreneur as being all-consuming. She says you can lose perspective if you work too hard, not seeing family and friends for periods of time if you're not careful. But having a dog means you are forced to take breaks and walk every day. There is no chance to cancel or say you are too busy because you know that your dog needs his walks.

Dogs change the energy in an office, encouraging staff to get up and move around – all of which benefits productivity. At Digital Mums, the presence of dogs in the office also creates daily amusement. The interaction between the two dogs is much more entertaining than watching TV, while lunchtime walks create opportunities for different team members to get together and chat away from the office space. The dogs can also be a great conversation starter, and it's not unusual for visitors to get their phones out to show photos of their own pets – a good icebreaker before a meeting.

Emotional support

Nikki says that having the two dogs in the office has a calming effect and a positive impact on any anxiety. Staff smile with them around and visitors get a very warm reception from the dogs who are always pleased to see anyone new.

In particular, Rolo has helped Nikki with worry and stress. When she gets up, he gets up, and he is by her side pretty much 24 hours a day, seven days a week. His manner is relaxed and very comforting, which impacts positively on her. They walk twice a day and both times, Nikki is 100 percent in the moment and very mindful that this is their walk time – so no phones or distractions, which means that both she and Rolo can switch off and enjoy the walk. Pre-dog, Nikki found this much harder to do. She jokes that she should get Rolo a little jacket that says "Emotional Support", as he has such a soothing effect.

ANIMALS AS THERAPY

Four bouncy, lively boys live in my house. One of them is in his 40s, but pretends that he is still young by skateboarding and generally joining in with the kids. They make endless noise, have incredible imaginations and are often seen recreating scenes from *Jurassic World*, *Star Wars* battles or making up random plays that evolve in their heads as they happen.

One of the boys has sensory issues and, as a result, can have mega-meltdowns. To the outsider, they may appear to come from nowhere, but we have a good idea of what triggers his zero-to-shouting in a matter of seconds.

He can sense when people are being fair and treating him with respect and when they are not. Most of the time he is right; the issue is his reaction, which can get him into trouble as it usually happens with quite some speed and volume. In the event of a tussle over a toy, say, he is the one who often gets told off, as he is the loudest and draws attention to himself.

We adore all of our children, and while this one has been the hardest personality to get to know due to his complexities, he is a kind, intelligent, creative, funny little soul. We surround him with love and have been working hard for the last three years to get support from professionals to help to teach him how to regulate himself a little better.

A therapy dog is one of the things that has been suggested to help calm my son during a meltdown. News to me. Dogs for the blind, supporting their owners to live as normal lives as possible, I am familiar with. There are fish in our dentist's waiting room, offering a sense of calm as patients hear the drilling coming from the next room. But animals are, in fact, being used in a variety of workplaces, schools and hospitals as therapy for people. And I had no idea.

We often look after our friend's dog and the family dynamic completely changes when we do. The door opens and the dog bounds in. The boys turn puppy-like with their energy and the whole place rocks a little with the bounding and chasing, ball throwing and barking. Then, when they settle into their mojo and the dog has tired itself out, a sense of calm falls over the house. The only other time this happens is when the kids are snuggled under blankets with us watching a movie or when they are sleeping.

The energy with a dog in the house is lovely. The boys are all kinder to each other, work more as a team and listen to us more; their instinct is to protect and care for the dog. I can see that the benefits to the entire family would be good, especially when one child has a big meltdown and the knock-on effect causes everyone some anxiety.

" "

HAVING THE TWO
DOGS IN THE OFFICE
HAS A CALMING
EFFECT AND A
POSITIVE IMPACT
ON ANY ANXIETY

I know the commitment is huge and my hands are already full with the three boys. But the more I look into it and learn about the incredible therapeutic benefits, the more convinced I am about getting a dog. Tales of families' lives being changed by the introduction of a therapy-trained dog are tear-jerking. When children with sensory issues experience fear or overwhelm, they often bolt and run off, but the dogs are trained to sit down when this happens, therefore encouraging the child to stay put, as they won't want to leave them.

A PET FOR LIFE

I began my research to see whether a dog could help my son with sensory needs. I am concluding it by looking for a dog for the whole family.

Animals clearly bring humour, calm and joy to people's lives on a daily basis. Goats in schools bring both staff and children together in a way that might not otherwise be possible. Dogs in the office break down barriers for those who may feel anxious, work too hard or need to take more breaks.

I can see that I would benefit from having a dog when I work from home. A dog would calm me as much as my son. Watch this space.

PAWS FOR THOUGHT

Animals for life

1 | TALK TO YOUR BOSS
Are pets allowed in your office? Take this book into work, leave it on the HR manager's desk, casually open on this chapter. Make the suggestion.

2 | HELPING HAND
The next time a friend is feeling ill or low, instead of offering to make them a meal or take them flowers, take your dog or cat round and watch the calming effect it has on them.

3 | VOLUNTEER
Become a volunteer and take your pet into schools or hospitals. There are several charities that can help train your pet to bring happiness to lots of people.

4 | DOG-LISTENING
Talk to your child's school. Dog therapy has such good feedback on reading; see if they know about it and suggest dogs for reading.

5 | VISIT SOME ANIMALS
There are some great zoos to visit animals and also farms. Lambing season is a good time to get into nature and connect with the animals around us.

6 | GET A PET?
Pets are a commitment both financially and timewise. But the mental-health benefits appear to be great and are well worth considering.

CHAPTER 9

BY MY SIDE

CHAPTER 9

BY MY SIDE

How animals keep us in touch with the world as we age

Clare Barry | Founder of Urban Curiosity

Recently, I had a four-day stay on an acute medical-care ward. I had been a hospital in-patient only once before that, and being so ill made me feel vulnerable and frightened. I was the youngest person in the bay and, through the haze of medication and anxiety, I picked up on how keen the Polish widow in the next bed was to get home to her beloved old beagle. She talked about him with such affection, and was desperate to prove to the doctors that she was well enough to leave. Later, a nurse told me how older people who owned pets tended to recover faster than those who did not. A large study in Sweden showed that people who lived alone with a dog were found to have a 33 percent reduced risk of death. This is due to a combination of factors: daily movement, sense of purpose and belonging, social connections and the calming impact of petting animals. As I accepted my temporary physical impairment and hoped for my own discharge date, I wondered whether the most important and unrecognized aspect of pet ownership in our twilight years is that they may preserve our dignity better than humans. Can we trust animals to honour our pride and look up to us, even if we can no longer walk so well or we get muddled about things?

THE POWER OF MEMORY AND STORIES

The ageing population is growing fast everywhere. A longer lifespan is wonderful, but chronic loneliness is a major problem and 70 percent of people in care homes have dementia or severe memory problems according to the UK's Alzheimer's Society. I am afraid of not knowing who I am more than of my eventual physical decline or experiencing isolation. Will I end up being fed apple purée in an unfamiliar place where no one knows my life story? I confess

" "

WE NEED TO BE
NEEDED; WE NEED
TO BE SEEN AND
CHERISHED

these anxieties to my friend Katie. "It's about a loss of independence and dignity," she decides. "Animals are a very calming presence. They know our stories and struggles intuitively, and I believe they can silently support us." As if she knows what we're talking about, Nell the collie, places her chin on Katie's lap and gazes up at her mistress with gentle brown eyes.

Ageing can mean a shift in, and shrinking of, our support network, while our physical and/or mental wellbeing become more fragile. Programmes like HenPower from the UK-based creative ageing charity Equal Arts help preserve the identity and stories of older people to keep connections open, which is beneficial for both body and mind. Equal Arts provides creative opportunities for older people and those living with dementia and other life-limiting conditions. A case in point, in 2012, the charity established HenPower to combine arts activities with hen-keeping in care settings, hospices, assisted-living schemes and schools to tackle social isolation, reduce depression and improve people's wellbeing.

"It's a life-transforming experience that brings people together around a whole mutual interest," says Glenda Cook, professor of nursing at the UK's Northumbria University. "There's such diversity in the project that people can find a space there. There could be a role for anyone, from the carpentry work through to looking after the hens themselves."

Volunteers – or "henshioners", as they like to be called – were also service-users and some of them were living independently, while others resided in care homes. "This quirky project captured the imagination," says Professor Cook, who led a 12-month study into the impact of the programme on participants in 2013. "They invest so much time and energy into it because it's about doing things together for a mutual cause that doesn't focus on problems or the ageing process. It's just really good fun!"

The majority of the community had kept hens in their younger years and there was something very familiar about it for that generation. "It brought all that reminiscence back and that connectivity across a life course," explains the professor. Those connections are vital in counteracting a sense of insecurity, loss or separation, and henshioners who had left pets behind or been widowed were able to transfer their caring skills to the hens. But the project was not just about the hens themselves. Service-users also participated in creative sessions. For example, they drew pictures of the hens and sang songs. It sounds right up my street.

In the case of people living with dementia, life can be fragmented, as their sense of self is disintegrating. Holding onto their stories, experiences and achievements is important in a confusing time. Professor Cook described a day when she was in the enclosed garden at a care home: "This lady sat down next to me and the hens kept appearing and reappearing from the bushes and, because her dementia was so advanced, it was like a new experience each time. The joy on her face!" Jos Forester-Melville, HenPower programme manager, told me about a woman with dementia at another UK care home. She said no one would sit next to her due to her aggressive behaviour: "She kept shouting out marching orders, 'Left, right, left, right', because she'd been very senior in the army. I went over and asked, 'Can I put this hen on your lap?' I wasn't sure what response I'd get, but she said, 'Oh I love hens. My mother used to keep hens.' I gave her the chicken and you could just see her shoulders drop – the tension drained away from her. There was an instant connection."

The HenPower evaluation showed improved health and wellbeing with a significant reduction in agitation and the use of anti-psychotic medication during the project. This supports the findings of world-leading dementia expert Professor Clive Ballard of the UK's University of Exeter medical school – namely, that connection, engagement and keeping our stories alive keeps *us* alive and well. Or at least that's my take on it. For me, the idea of having new experiences and meeting new people right up until the day I die is important.

Henshioners come from a generation that did not have the same chance to go on to higher education as I did. Each year, a group of them visit a university campus to share the HenPower story with third-year nursing undergraduates. Many of the henshioners could never have imagined being given the title of visiting lecturer at this stage in their lives. This new identity and the experience of going into the university and local schools has given them a credibility and opportunities they just wouldn't otherwise have had. And they're playing an important role in helping to shape future generations for the better.

" "

KEEPING OUR
STORIES ALIVE
KEEPS US ALIVE
AND WELL

Geriatric nursing is not very popular, but Professor Cook and her team want to spark a change in that.

On the first day of term, the henshioners bring chicks to meet the students and give a lecture. "Most of the group end up with tears rolling down their faces and they tell us it's the best lecture they have over the three years. It changes their attitude," explains Professor Cook. "The thing is, nurses see people at a vulnerable point in their life. In this case, rather than seeing someone who is sick, they see these older people making a great contribution to society and building positive relationships within the community."

"CAN WE TRUST ANIMALS TO HONOUR OUR PRIDE AND LOOK UP TO US, EVEN IF WE CAN NO LONGER WALK SO WELL OR WE GET MUDDLED ABOUT THINGS?"

Equal Arts' HenPower connects communities and crosses generational boundaries. It shows there is much to discover, learn and love as we get older. HenPower has spread, with more and more people now benefitting from the calming presence of these feathered animals. I am heartened to learn the men and women engaged in this programme are not lonely or sitting in a day room feeling ignored.

Katie wants to end her days in a care home with a collie and a miniature donkey at her feet. I'd be happy with some painting sessions, egg-collecting and exercising my vocal cords with a round or two of the traditional children's song "Chick-chick-chick-chicken".

THE IMPORTANCE OF COMPANIONSHIP AND IDENTITY
"Care homes and hospitals are the most human yet the least human places. They terrify me," admits Katie. "My beautiful grandma had a series of strokes after my grandfather died. I remember visiting her in a place where everything seemed plastic and antiseptic. All the textures, lighting, monitors, drips,

plastic-covered chairs and wipe-clean mattresses – it was not dissimilar in look to a prison. And the overly cheery staff in brightly coloured aprons shouted personal questions: 'Do you need the toilet, Mrs Mason?'"

Though there is a good reason for these sterile environments, the identity of a woman whose life was filled with purpose and people got lost somewhere between her husband's passing and her own ill health.

Katie's grandmother, Mary Mason, worked as a midwife in post-war Britain, when conditions for delivering babies were tough. She suffered greatly with anxiety and was sent to a farm in the north of England for respite care. There, she fell in love with the owner and together they raised four children. Mary fed the family and workers. She kept chickens and filled the chest freezer with the piles of fruit her husband had grown to make delicious pies year-round. She loved to entertain: everyone from vicars to feed salespeople, peace-prize-winners to Dutch cyclists sat at her table. She was proud of these visits and noted them all in a diary.

Katie gets melancholic remembering how her grandmother – the farm matriarch and the glue that kept everyone together – became a tiny old lady in a high-back chair. "It made me wonder about the stories of the other people in the room. I am thoroughly ashamed to say that all I could see was brutal decay and frailty. Is this our human coping mechanism to allow the world to keep on moving?"

I wonder if, when Mary was widowed, she struggled with the lack of responsibility for something or someone other than herself after years of being a farmer's wife, housekeeper and hostess. She would have loved – and benefitted from – being involved with HenPower.

We need to be needed; we need to be seen and cherished. I shiver at the memory of my aunt telling me how entering middle age made her feel invisible. I don't want to feel insignificant or a burden to my loved ones in the future. For many men, this sense of being unseen by the world often comes in retirement and can hurt intensely. Certainly, in my own grandfather's case, life after work meant a loss of identity and purpose, pride and earning power.

There is less pressure to be jolly or put a brave face on things with a pet. "It's easy to make a dog wag its tail and it's so satisfying," she continues. "I can't help but smile a little when Nell is so delighted with my attention. The gentle companionship of Nell can pull me out of myself."

NAVIGATING TRANSITION AND PRESERVING OUR DIGNITY

I reconsider Katie's recommendation that I get a canine of my own. Then I panic: what happens, then, when life circumstances force me to part ways with my (theoretical) beloved pooch?

"Having to leave your home when circumstances dictate due to frailty and/or disability is a traumatic enough experience, but having to also leave your pet – often, your reason for living – is unthinkable," says Mrs Averil Jarvis MBE, chief executive of the UK's Cinnamon Trust, a charity dedicated to helping people who are terminally ill or elderly to care for their pets when they no longer can. It also provides long-term care for pets whose owners have died or moved to residential accommodation.

Mrs Jarvis founded the charity in 1985 and named it after her beloved corgi. The trust now has a network of 16,000 volunteers who, in the year to March 2017 helped 84,376 people and 91,254 animals. I love the idea of daily walks for the cocker spaniel whose master is housebound, or a clean cage for the rabbit with an owner who is about to be discharged from hospital. I well up when Mrs Jarvis describes how volunteers foster animals and the trust facilitates permanent care for those whose owners are terminally ill. It must be a great comfort to know your faithful furry or feathered companion will be loved and well looked after when you're gone.

Some people making the transition between independent and supported living take their animals with them into residential care. Each year, the Cinnamon Trust awards prizes to pet-friendly care homes. Louise Turner, manager of one such home, tells me how one resident has mild dementia and gets confused. "But her little dog is her companion and constant presence. It understands her ways." Given my fear of losing my mental faculties as I age, I am relieved there are places where Dolly (my fantasy Dachshund) would be welcome.

Maybe animals can reconnect older people with the world outside too and help them retain the essence of who they were before the passage of time took its toll. These creatures may be a passport back to the wonky, imperfect community of which their owners were once a part. They live in the moment and don't worry about the future or if we might die tomorrow. They are simply here now, and they look up to us even when we feel tiny.

When I think about it, the loyalty and lack of judgment our animals show is hugely helpful at a time when our memories might be failing or we find it hard to get our socks on. Exposing our frailty in front of a human might make us feel self-conscious or patronized; our four-legged friends will never make us feel that way. They lift our spirits just by their presence and offer a dignity and patience that others don't give us.

SENSORY DELIGHT

Louise Turner mentions something else: the power of touch. If getting older increases the likelihood of loneliness and a lack of human contact, then sensory deprivation will be missing too. We have a chemical as well as an emotional need for touch. It soothes us and helps us to bond and connect with each other. When we experience touch, we feel relaxed, connected and calm, as the love hormone, oxytocin, rockets and the stress hormone, cortisol, drops.

According to psychologist Miriam Akhtar, touch "activates the orbitofrontal cortex in the brain, which is linked to feelings of reward and empathy, making us more optimistic and less cynical or suspicious of others. It speeds recovery times from illness and surgery, aids digestion and boosts survival rates of patients with complex diseases. Alzheimer's patients do better with nurturing touch therapies, such as massage, than without." This is echoed by a study that found that people who experience minimal human contact in a care setting are 64 percent more likely to develop clinical dementia. Meanwhile, Professor Clive Ballard has discovered that many residents in care homes receive as little as two minutes of social interaction a day. In a TV interview, he said that social activities were often in groups, for example, bingo, and that many residents were not engaged.

KATIE AND CLARE AT STEPNEY CITY FARM

In recognition of this potential disengagement, the importance of sensory delight and the fact that the majority of Louise Turner's residents come from an agricultural or farming background, she and her colleague Jan have created an inspiring events programme. I'm so relieved to hear it because I have visions of being stuck in a high-backed chair – like Katie's beloved grandma – with empty hours unfurling in front of me. I might be living in London now, but perhaps I'll retire to the countryside and, when the time comes, join Louise's gang, stroking guinea pigs and rabbits. "They are warm, soft and comforting to hold, but the bigger four-legged need to be patted," she says. "The llamas' eyelashes are a big talking point! We take them around the grounds and also into the rooms of immobile residents to enjoy them too. I love seeing the smiles on residents' faces. They reminisce and connect with each other and the staff in a different way."

I love the idea of llamas in my bedroom when my legs won't let me get out and about. It would beat daytime TV. Plus, every Easter, Jan brings in chicks she's been incubating at home. "Visits from animals are therapeutic generally: touch and engagement can soothe and brighten up a resident's mood and lift them from boredom or an anxious state," she explains.

A few things strike me when Louise and Jan are talking: this is an activity with appeal for men and women; it encourages movement and use of the care home's gardens; the residents talk about the visits for days after the animals are gone. Typical care-home activities lean more toward creative pursuits like knitting or painting that don't always interest the male population and tend not to involve getting out in the fresh air. These animals unite the home's community and promote mental and physical wellbeing, connection and happiness. Perhaps I have nothing to worry about getting old or losing my marbles, after all.

Animals can be a potent presence in our lives. They can enhance our happiness and sense of wellbeing as we navigate the twists and turns of a lifetime. I feel more hopeful about my twilight years and I make a pact with Katie: we're going to end our days in the same place, where we'll remember the old stories and make new ones. There'll definitely be a collie, but I'm not sure about the miniature donkey or the dachshund.

PAWS FOR THOUGHT

Growing old gracefully with an animal by your side

1 | A FURRY ANCHOR

Having an animal by one's side, whether it's a pet or a borrowed creature, is soothing and reassuring in a time of uncertainty or change.

2 | BESIDE PEACE

An animal's peaceful presence brings us into the here and now and allows us to leave worries or anxieties behind for a while.

3 | IT'S ALL GOOD

The eyes of a furry friend see no wrong. Just being loved without being judged for the many ways our minds and bodies age can provide a much-needed lift, returning life's lightness.

4 | STILL NEEDED

Taking care of another being gives a life-affirming sense of being needed. As time passes and other ways in which we were needed might lessen, then the care of a pet provides a wonderful sense of purpose.

5 | CARING TOGETHER

When a group of elders care for animals together the fun of a shared sense of purpose offers laughter and a reaffirming of self-worth.

6 | LIGHT TOUCH

Touch lifts the mood, and petting, cuddling and caring for a pet lifts a low mood. A little lightness can be brought to daily life with this physical connection.

CHAPTER 10

GETTING

HOOKED

[content warning: depression/suicidal thoughts]

GETTING HOOKED

Finding a way forward with your pet

Sophie Rickard | Psychologist, Writer, Author of *Mann's Best Friend*

I am a hopeless cliché.

My children are growing up, moving out, and I am filling the house with baby animals. It's getting out of hand. To be frank, I'm waiting for someone to put their foot down, to tell me to stop. But who?

It started with dog-sitting, the gateway drug to a house full of pets. We had Charlie to stay so often it began to feel odd when he wasn't around. Like there was a dog-shaped hole in our lives. So we got a puppy. Jessie, a Border collie, grew to be a dog who lives to herd things, whether you ask her to or not. It therefore seemed only natural to get her half a dozen Indian runner ducks to play with. The incubator and hatchery were a small step from there. She now has 14 ducks and the lawn is a travesty. And did I mention the fish? They don't say much, but they are pretty. Now, what I would really like is a lovely black and white cat, but I can't have one. Jessie would strongly object, and I'm not sure how it would go down with any ducklings either. I'm being brave about not getting a cat. I have taken my mind off it by introducing Jessie to a handsome stud collie. We shall have puppies soon!

See what I mean?

OWNERSHIP

I'm a bit squeamish about the title "dog owner". I use it, and I understand how it is helpful. But surely we serve our animals, not the other way around? OK, you might have paid cash for the rabbit in the pet shop (along with his two-storey

" "

IT'S HARD
TO BE A FRIEND
TO SOMEONE WHO'S
DEPRESSED, BUT IT IS
ONE OF THE KINDEST,
NOBLEST AND BEST
THINGS YOU WILL
EVER DO

Stephen Fry

hutch and the feeders and the cool toys), but we all know he's no asset. From the minute he moves in, you wait on him and you fulfil his needs: the daily rounds of food, water and exercise; endless mucking out; popping out for more hay, sawdust, food, special vitamins... It is all part of the joy of pets. In what way does *he* belong to *you*? He's just letting you think that.

"PEOPLE ARE RESPONSIBLE FOR THE HEALTH OF THE LAND AND THE WATER THAT NURTURES THEM"

The indigenous people of Australia had a very different concept of property and ownership to the European settlers. Aboriginal tradition never conceived of land as an asset to be traded or owned, but as a care – the people are responsible for the health of the land and the water that nurtures them. The land is a mother, and we, the children of the land, have care and respect for the mother's health and vitality. This is the relationship we have with pets. And it can be lifesaving.

DANGEROUS THINKING

British actor and writer Stephen Fry said, "It's hard to be a friend to someone who's depressed, but it is one of the kindest, noblest and best things you will ever do."

Depression is a self-fulfilling prophecy of doom, stitched together with misery and despair. If you've ever been anywhere near it, you'll recognize the pit of empty, hopeless sadness, insomnia, guilt, self-hatred and feeling of utter, utter pointlessness that depression digs into your life. The pit is deep, with slippery walls that offer no foothold. It is lonely and, apparently, permanent. But depression lies.

When I was at my lowest point, depression had me believing that my family would be better off if I was dead. I thought I had become a malignant influence on my children, and that I was harming them with my toxicity. There was a very fragile veneer of rational thought helping me to hide this from the rest of the world, and a level on which I knew my thinking was terribly wrong – but knowing this did not help.

The idea that recovery, or redemption, was possible was unimaginable at that time. But I'm better now. So much so that I am in a position to counsel others. I got better gradually. Lots of things have contributed. My daughter saw what I was going through, and put in my hands Sylvia Plath's 1961 poem "Tulips". It is not a cheery read, to be sure, but it was exactly what I needed. It introduced me to the painful but lifesaving concept of "hooks". The line, describing a family photo, goes:

.....

their smiles catch onto my skin, little smiling hooks

.....

And that is how I felt. I felt pierced by my daughter's understanding. I felt barbed by the love and care of those around me. And I began to use the hooks and barbs to entangle the nets that helped me climb out of the pit.

Some of the greatest hooks have four legs. Or even two muddy legs and a beak.

A WAY FORWARD

Jessie and her flock have helped me to help myself through, among other things, the incredible motivator that is fulfilling the needs of others. One symptom of depression is a total lack of interest in any kind of self-care. What is the point in investing in yourself, when you are held in such low regard? Why would you have your hair cut, or get new clothes, or eat nice food? And from there, it doesn't take long before you get to why brush your hair, get dressed, or eat at all? Any slight attempt to act for your own good seems like a ridiculous indulgence. But there was nothing that made me jump out of bed quite like the sound of a puppy in digestive distress.

" "

SOME OF THE
GREATEST HOOKS
HAVE FOUR LEGS.
OR EVEN TWO
MUDDY LEGS
AND A BEAK

In 2010, middle-aged American Eric O'Grey weighed 154 kg (24 stone), and was using 15 different medications every day including insulin, antidepressants and weight-loss drugs. "I just felt miserable all the time," O'Grey explained. "It's just amazing how painful it is to be that heavy." Eric consulted a naturopath, who prescribed two things: a wholefood, plant-based diet and the adoption of a shelter dog. Out of ideas and desperate to change his life, he followed her odd instructions.

The shelter assigned Eric an obese dog with skin problems, which was not what he'd had in mind. Peety looked equally disappointed in Eric. They started with walks of about 90 metres. Eric really struggled, but Peety seemed so grateful that it motivated him to keep going. As the walks got longer, and they explored the neighbourhood together, Eric found that Peety was a great conversation starter. "I decided to become the person who he thought I was. And over time, really every part of my life improved. I was so reclusive and removed from society at the time that I needed a relationship in my life." Eric is now a healthy weight, married, running marathons and writing. His book is called *Walking with Peety: The Dog Who Saved My Life*.

145

Stories like this are exciting to me, because Peety opened doors for Eric to take part in his own life more fully. Peety didn't change Eric, but he facilitated his growth from a position of sadness and ill health, to one of fulfilment and creativity. And the first thing Peety did was to get Eric outside. But this is complicated for me.

OUTDOORS FOR THE DISINCLINED

While I completely sign up to the noble idea of a "nature cure", I remain averse to leaving the house. My natural introversion combined with a painful, chronic health condition, and a whiff of legacy agoraphobia and social phobia from the breakdown, seem to conspire to keep me at my desk. This might help productivity, but it does my health no good at all.

Exercise, improved circulation, fresh air, taking in the subtle miracles of the changing seasons and the force of nature are certainly good for my peace of mind. Anxiety, chronic pain and money worries are not so much reasons to stay in, as the very things that make going out necessary. I grumble about doing it, but I always come back happier. And I have learned some tricks:

- If I don't want to meet people, I choose to go out in the rain.

- The same walk every day is not boring – the subtle seasonal developments are incredible.

- If my mind is too busy to enjoy walking, I blast loud classical music through headphones – and accept any applause on the recordings for myself.

- If I can't manage a walk, there is entertainment enough in 1m² of closely examined garden, park or hedgerow.

- If I can't get outside, a window bird feeder (or a fish tank or a hamster in his cage) offers a similar sense of quiet peace and awe at the miracle of life.

Animals force us to live in the moment. They need us to put aside any problematic past, troubling future, impending doom or existential dread in order to serve their very real and immediate physical needs. This replaces rumination with constructive actions, even if only for a few minutes. Yes, it's good to think about the things that worry you, but it's also good to take a break occasionally. There is nothing quite like picking up warm poo through a plastic bag to bring you down to earth in a positive, life-affirming way.

WHO NEEDS IT?

My story might seem dramatic, but it's not as unusual as you might think. It's difficult to talk about this kind of stuff, so we can never know who among us might be going through something similar. But going by the extraordinary success of British novelist and journalist Matt Haig's 2015 book, *Reasons to Stay Alive*, a lot of people are looking for support and encouragement with this kind of problem.

In one of the chapters in that book – "#reasonstostayalive" – Matt explains that he opened up the question "What keeps you going?" to his vast Twitter

" "

WHEN YOUR LIFE
IS PRECARIOUS AND
CHALLENGING, YET YOU
MANAGE TO PROVIDE
SOME SIMPLE SECURITY
FOR YOUR ANIMAL,
IT IS REWARDED WITH
GRATITUDE, CONSISTENT
AFFECTION AND LOVE

following, many of whom have experience of depression, anxiety or suicidal thoughts. Spending time with pets, their love and devotion and their neediness made up one in ten of the of the replies to this broad question.

The 18th-century British poet and abolitionist William Cowper made three attempts on his own life, was institutionalized for a couple of years, then, ten years later, slid into a horrific five-year depression. His recovery has been attributed to his vigorous Christianity – and he did knock together some smashing hymns. And the writer G K Chesterton suggested he crawled out of it by writing comic verse ("poetry was not the disease, but the medicine"). But how about this? A turning point came when a neighbour foisted a neglected pet leveret on him. Cowper, who was apparently "glad of anything that would engage his attention without fatiguing it", found the hare-raising suited him very well. He collected more leverets, loved them, wrote poems and stories about them, and, through them, found small ways to enjoy life again.

For those of us with chaotic lives, the introduction of another species can provide a helpful organizing principle. An orderly routine, and the grounding nature of the predictable needs and responses of a pet, can help us manage chaos differently. If your sleep patterns are in tatters, the dog will keep you tethered to time with her meal- and walk times. When your life is precarious and challenging, yet you manage to provide some simple security for your animal, it is rewarded with gratitude, consistent affection and love.

At the other end of the scale, for those of us with restricted lives, sharing our world with an animal can introduce vibrancy, fun and spontaneity. Pets are not programmable; however thoroughly well trained, they retain agency over their thoughts and actions. That's right, he's *choosing* to roll over and play dead on command, because he wants to please you. Playing is good for all of us. And to receive spontaneous affection from another creature can be life changing. Enough to constitute a hook with which to climb upward.

EVERYDAY HEROES
We've all heard amazing stories about brave animals that have saved people's lives in remarkable circumstances – they are interspecies heroes. But, much

like their human counterparts, there are hundreds of thousands of animals out there saving lives in less dramatic ways all the time, by being their ordinary everyday selves. Peety saved Eric's life by needing exercise. Others do it by staying still.

Take the Cat Rule, for example. By this, I mean that moment when you *would* answer the door/make the tea/whatever, but the cat is sleeping on your lap. The Cat Rule is an unwritten commandment that no person, no matter how much they might want a glass of water or to charge their phone, may disturb a cat that has chosen to sleep on them. This is the gift of still, calm peace, delivered in a warm, purring package. It keeps you still. It keeps you alive. Pets keep your feet on the ground amid whatever whirlwind of stress you might be experiencing.

You may have picked up that I have a tendency toward gloom, a habit that extends to my reading preferences. My husband once took the children to a bookshop to choose a birthday present for me, and the sales assistant was startled to hear a chirpy seven-year-old explain, "What Mum likes is the ones where everyone dies in the end". I also like value for money (an excuse for reading ridiculously long books). So Victor Hugo's *Les Misérables* is an obvious favourite. Yet the best line in it is remarkably optimistic:

....

To love another person is to see the face of God.

.....

I'm not religious, but I do have faith. My faith is in people. And I think what Hugo means in that line (which made it into the record-breaking stage musical) is that to feel love for another person is to understand the miracle of life. To "see the face of God", by my interpretation, means to experience that overpowering motivation to live and to fulfil your own dreams; to realize the vital beauty in the tiny spark of the universe that is your life, and to want to keep that spark alive. And the innocence, trust and purity of the love between people and their pets can also show us "the face of God".

JESSIE'S PURPOSE

The pure joy with which Jessie and her flock greet each day challenges any reflexive gloom. The relentless day-in-day-out neediness that she dedicates to me is overwhelming. I can't stay in bed all day now; I can't even stay indoors. It starts before daybreak, as she hassles us to let her ducks out earlier and earlier each morning. She taps her ceramic bowl politely but insistently at 8am, 1pm and 6pm. She prompts us at dusk to put the ducks away, safe from the fox. She's scared of the dark, but she prowls the perimeter anyway, reminding the fox to keep away. These things happen every day, without fail. It doesn't matter what mood I'm in, or what else I might be struggling with, that bowl will be tapped. And I will answer the tap – because however bad I have felt so far, that hook has snagged me.

Although it is technically possible for a human and an animal to live together and have little to do with one another, if you are the person responsible for meeting the needs of that creature, I expect you have a remarkably complex relationship; one in which it is unclear who needs who the most. Like with all relationships, we get out what we put in. And so do they.

When Jessie's pups are born, she and I will work together to give them a safe and loving start in life. Hopefully, they will go on to live on farms and train for the purpose of the breed – sheep herding. They will live fulfilling lives in close partnership with a shepherd whose objective is to work with them.

One of the pups will stay here with us, and learn from Jessie how to care for a small flock of filthy ducks, warm my feet and support my writing. It's a funny sort of purpose for a collie dog, but I know one who is very good at it. And I am hooked on her.

PAWS FOR THOUGHT

Appreciating purpose with your pet

1 | THE FUTURE NOW
Time is just a load of Now linked together in a chain. You only need to survive the present moment; let the next one look after itself.

2 | OWN YOUR PEDESTAL
Can you live up to the image your pets have of you? Peety put Eric on a pedestal, so Eric aimed to deserve it.

3 | LOOK FOR HOOKS
Different things hook different people. What is your greatest motivation to take part in your own life? Where can you find your hook when you need one?

4 | PAY ATTENTION
Enjoy every moment with all your senses, especially the mundane physical tasks your animal demands of you. Think of mucking out as a break from humankind.

5 | BE STILL
Observe the Cat Rule. Let yourself be chosen for peace and tranquility. Luxuriate in them.

6 | PLAY
Play games with your pets, have fun, laugh together. Give them a task, and enjoy helping them undertake it (but don't get more than six ducks if you like your garden).

EXTRAS

REFERENCES, RESOURCES AND CREDITS

REFERENCES

All websites accessed January 2018

Chapter 1

Rogers, C. R. (June 6, 1956) "The Necessary and Sufficient Conditions of Therapeutic Personality Change". *Journal of Consulting Psychology*, Vol. 21, pp. 95–103

Flanagan, J. (2000) "Lovebirds transform South Africa's hardest criminals". *The Telegraph*

Havey, J., Vlasses, F., Vlasses, P., Ludwig-Beymer, P. and Hackbarth, D. (2014) "The Effect of Animal-Assisted Therapy on Pain Medication Use After Joint Replacement". *Anthrozoös*, 27(3), 361–9

Mearns, D., Thorne, B. and McLeod, J. (2013) *Person-Centred Counselling In Action*, Sage Publications

Melson, G., Kahn Jr, P., Beck, A and Friedman, B. (2009) "Robotic Pets in Human Lives: Implications for the Human–Animal Bond and for Human Relationships with Personified Technologies". *Journal Of Social Issues*, 65(3), 545–67

Mubanga, M., Byberg, L., Nowak, C., Egenvall, A., Magnusson, P., Ingelsson, E. and Fall, T.. (2017) *"Dog ownership and the risk of cardiovascular disease and death – a nationwide cohort study"*. *Scientific Reports*, 7(1)

Nagasawa, M., Mitsui, S., Shiori E., Ohtani, N., Ohta, M. and Sakuma, Y. et al. (2015) "Oxytocin-gaze positive loop and the coevolution of human-dog bonds". *Science*, 348 (6232), pp.333–6

Chapter 2

www.time.com/4728315/science-says-pet-good-for-mental-health/

www.npr.org/2017/11/03/561551389/from-fire-hydrants-to-rescue-work-dogs-perceive-the-world-through-smell

www.animalcognition.org/2016/10/12/can-dogs-tell-time/

Chapter 3

go.roberts.edu/leadingedge/the-great-choices-of-strategic-leaders

news.un.org/en/story/2017/03/554462-some-300-million-people-suffer-depression-un-warns-ahead-world-health-day

Wood, D. (1999) *The Tao of Meow*, Bantam Doubleday Dell Publishing Group

uk.businessinsider.com/psychology-of-cat-videos-study-2015-6?r=US&IR=T

www.bbc.co.uk/news/magazine-37199653

www.huffingtonpost.co.uk/entry/the-surprising-reason-humans-love-cat-videos_us_55df58f9e4b029b3f1b1f693

www.instagram.com/choupettesdiary/?hl=en

www.instagram.com/smoothiethecat/?hl=en

www.instagram.com/realgrumpycat/?hl=en

www.bbc.co.uk/newsround/33848745

www.nytimes.com/2015/08/07/arts/design/how-cats-took-over-the-internet-at-the-museum-of-the-moving-image.html

uk.businessinsider.com/psychology-of-cat-videos-study-2015-6?r=US&IR=T

www.lolcats.com/

Chapter 5

Dosa, Dr D. (2011) *Making Rounds with Oscar: The Inspirational Story of a Doctor, His Patients and a Very Special Cat,* Headline Publishing Group

Dosa, Dr D. (July 26, 2007) "A day in the life of Oscar the Cat", *New England Journal of Medicine*

Speak Dog with Ali. "We need to bake the cake before icing it...". www.speakdogwithali.co.uk/what-i-do/

Chapter 6

Serpell, J. A. (2000) *"Creatures of the unconscious: Companion animals as mediators".* in Podberscek, A. L., Paul, E. S., & Serpell J. A. (Eds.), *Companion Animals and Us: Exploring the Relationship Between People and Pets.* pp.108–124. Cambridge University Press

Atlas Obscura. "Athena the Owl at the Florence Nightingale Museum". www.atlasobscura.com/places/athena-florence-nightingales-owl

Boris Levinson in Renck Jalongo, M., et al. (2004) "Canine Visitors: The Influence of Therapy Dogs on Young Children's Learning and Well-Being in Classrooms and Hospitals". *Early Childhood Education Journal* (32) 1, 9–16

Levinson, E. M., et al. (2017) "Effects of Reading with Adult Tutor/Therapy Dog Teams on Elementary Students' Reading Achievement and Attitudes". *Society & Animals.* 25, 38–56

Serpell, J A. (2000) "Creatures of the unconscious: Companion animals as mediators". in A. L. Podberscek, E. S. Paul, & J.A. Serpell (Eds.), *Companion animals and us: Exploring the relationship between people and pets.* Cambridge University Press

Chapter 7

www.psychologytoday.com/blog/between-cultures/201704/belonging

www.irishtimes.com/life-and-style/health-family/parenting/the-importance-of-relationships-and-belonging-1.3405948

www.youtube.com/watch?v=KSXh1YfNyVA&t=129s

www.ncbi.nlm.nih.gov/pmc/articles/PMC3489271/

Chapter 8

Google dog policy. "11 famous companies with enviable pet friendly policies". www.fastcompany.com/3037384/11-famous-companies-with-enviable-pet-friendly-policies

Varndean Goats. www.varndean.co.uk/goats

Chapter 9

www.time.com/5028171/health-benefits-owning-dog

www.independent.co.uk/news/health/dog-ownership-owners-live-longer-pets-cardiovascular-health-active-walking-research-study-finds-a8059976.html

www.theconversation.com/four-ways-having-a-pet-increases-your-lifespan-88640

www.telegraph.co.uk/beauty/skin/youthful-vitality/the-power-of-touch

www.theoldvicarage-leigh.co.uk

www.rd.com/health/wellness/company-of-hens

Chapter 10

Chillag, A. C. (2018). "How an overweight

shelter dog saved a man's life". CNN. www.
edition.cnn.com/2017/12/26/health/
dog-walking-exercise-saves-life/index.html

Chesterton, G K. (2012) *Orthodoxy*. Simon
& Brown

Haig, M. (2016) *Reasons To Stay Alive*. Thorpe

Hugo, V. (1982). *Les Misérables*, Penguin
Classics

Plath, S. (2015) *Ariel*, Faber & Faber

"Stephen Fry at 60: the polymath's wisest and
wittiest quotes" (2018). *The Telegraph*. www.
telegraph.co.uk/men/thinking-man/stephen-
frys-best-quotes/stephen-fry-quotes17/

Taylor, T. (1833) *The Life of William Cowper,
Esq.* Seeley & Burnside

RESOURCES

Pet-therapy services
Bark and Read Programme (UK)
Borrow My Doggy
Cinnamon Trust (UK)
Digital Mums
Explore by Paw (UK)
HenPower/Equal Arts (UK)
LOLCats
The Kennel Club
Varndean Goats

TEDx Talk: "The Simple Cure for
Loneliness"
Baya Voce TEDxSaltLake City

Websites
www.petsastherapy.org
Ways for you and your pet to get involved
with offering therapy or to seek out therapy
with pets.

www.moretodogstrust.org.uk/freedom-
project/freedom-project
A specialist service offering pet fostering for
people fleeing domestic violence.

www.rspca.org/findapet/foster
Find out about how to foster pets for the
RSPCA.

www.habri.org
An inspirational source of the latest thinking
and research at the Human Animal Bond
Research Institute, based in the USA.

www.assistancedogs.org.uk
A voluntary coalition of assistance-dog
organizations in the UK.

www.walkiees.co.uk
Share and discover the best dog walks in the
UK.

www.leapequine.com
Discover an accredited equine therapist near
you in the UK.

www.meetup.com/topics/dog-walks
Find dog-related meet-up groups.

Books
Dosa, Dr D. (2011) *Making Rounds with Oscar:
The Extraordinary Gift of an Ordinary Cat.*
Hyperion Books

Germer, C. K. (2009) *The Mindful Path to
Self-Compassion.* The Guilford Press

Haig, M. (2015) *Reasons to Stay Alive.*
Canongate Books

Neff, K. (2011) *Self Compassion: Stop Beating Yourself Up and Leave Insecurity Behind.*
Hodder & Stoughton

O'Grey, E., & Dagostino, M. (2017) *Walking with Peety The Dog Who Saved My Life.* Grand Central Publishing.

Pariser, E. (2012) *The Filter Bubble: What the Internet Is Hiding from You.* Penguin

Wax, R. (2016) *A Mindfulness Guide for the Frazzled.* Penguin

CREDITS

Thank you to our talented authors, artists and designers who agree that four legs can carry the most rewarding and unexpected therapeutic opportunities:

Sophie Rickard
www.gluepotbooks.com
Psychologist and writer. Author of *Mann's Best Friend* and co-founder of Gluepot Books.

Caroline O'Donoghue
www.czaroline.com
Contributing editor for The Pool, author of *Promising Young Women* and commissioning editor for London-based art website White Noise.

Clare Barry
www.urbancuriosity.co.uk
Founder of Urban Curiosity, a wellness and creativity company that helps busy people slow down and see things differently.

Rabbi Jonathan Wittenberg
www.jonathanwittenberg.org
Author of *Things My Dog Has Taught Me: About being a better human*, as well as many beautiful books about the Jewish faith and a life well lived.

Kate Peers
www.madabouttheboys.net
Writer, journalist and contributor in *The Mother Book* by Selfish Mother, as well as contributor in our other titles *Walking In The Rain* and *Washing Up Is Good For You.*

Dr Brennan Jacoby
www.philosophyatwork.co.uk
Founder of Philosophy at Work, trust expert and consultant philosopher specializing in making the complex clear.

Photography: James Champion
www.jch.format.com
London-based lifestyle and fashion photographer, dedicated to creativity and his cat, Bob.

Illustration: Veronica Wood
www.veronicawood.co.uk
Her best friends are her bottle of ink and a dip pen. Touching honesty and raw emotion shine through her illustrations.

Design and creative direction: Supafrank
www.supafrank.com
Katie Steel runs a collaborative design studio, developing brands that speak to real human beings.

NOTES

THANKS, NELL